PRAISE FOR

The Southern Girl's Guide to Surviving the Newlywed Years

"Annabelle Robertson will not only keep you sane—she'll keep you in stitches! It's a downright shame I didn't have this book before and during all of my marriages! My exes, bless their hearts, would have been grateful."

> —*Deborah Ford*, New York Times *bestselling*
> *author of* The GRITS (Girls Raised in
> the South) Guide to Life *and* Puttin' on
> the Grits

"With The *Southern Girl's Guide*, Annabelle Robertson takes her rightful place among the wise and witty Southern women of letters. Y'all buy this book and pay attention to everything she says."

> —*Dorothea Benton Frank*, New York Times
> *bestselling author of* Full of Grace *and*
> Pawleys Island

continued . . .

"Reading Annabelle Robertson's *Southern Girl's Guide* is like sitting on the front porch in uproarious laughter with your best friend while you discuss the joys and travails of married life from a uniquely Southern perspective. Annabelle has the uncanny ability to make us laugh at the funniest thing of all—the truth."

> —*Patti Callahan Henry, national bestselling author of* When Light Breaks *and* Where the River Runs

"Women, Southern or not, will know of 'wince' these ladies speak. Practical and humorous. This book has it all."

> —*Ronda Rich, national bestselling author of* What Southern Women Know (That Every Woman Should)

"Witty and wise. A real shot in the arm for avoiding the marital doldrums."

> —*Haywood Smith,* New York Times *bestselling author of* The Red Hat Club *and* The Red Hat Club Rides Again

"Combines down-home Southern wisdom with a modern woman's discerning wit. Funny and always surprising!"

> —*W. Bruce Cameron,* New York Times *bestselling author of* How to Remodel a Man *and* 8 Simple Rules for Dating My Teenage Daughter

"Don't read *The Southern Girl's Guide to Surviving the Newlywed Years* while eating grits or they'll end up coming out your nose."

> —*Tim Bete, author of* In The Beginning . . . There Were No Diapers *and director of the Erma Bombeck Writers' Workshop*

The Southern Girl's Guide
to Surviving the Newlywed Years

How to Stay Sane Once You've Caught Your Man

Annabelle Robertson

THE
Southern Girl's Guide
TO SURVIVING THE
Newlywed Years

 NEW AMERICAN LIBRARY

New American Library
Published by New American Library, a division of
Penguin Group (USA) Inc., 375 Hudson Street,
New York, New York 10014, USA
Penguin Group (Canada), 90 Eglinton Avenue East, Suite 700, Toronto,
Ontario M4P 2Y3, Canada (a division of Pearson Penguin Canada Inc.)
Penguin Books Ltd., 80 Strand, London WC2R 0RL, England
Penguin Ireland, 25 St. Stephen's Green, Dublin 2,
Ireland (a division of Penguin Books Ltd.)
Penguin Group (Australia), 250 Camberwell Road, Camberwell, Victoria 3124,
Australia (a division of Pearson Australia Group Pty. Ltd.)
Penguin Books India Pvt. Ltd., 11 Community Centre, Panchsheel Park,
New Delhi - 110 017, India
Penguin Group (NZ), cnr Airborne and Rosedale Roads, Albany,
Auckland 1310, New Zealand (a division of Pearson New Zealand Ltd.)
Penguin Books (South Africa) (Pty.) Ltd., 24 Sturdee Avenue,
Rosebank, Johannesburg 2196, South Africa

Penguin Books Ltd., Registered Offices:
80 Strand, London WC2R 0RL, England

First published by New American Library,
a division of Penguin Group (USA) Inc.

First Printing, January 2007
10   9   8   7   6   5   4   3   2   1

 REGISTERED TRADEMARK—MARCA REGISTRADA

LIBRARY OF CONGRESS CATALOGING-IN-PUBLICATION DATA

Robertson, Annabelle.
The Southern girl's guide to surviving the newlywed years: how to stay sane once you've caught
your man/Annabelle Robertson.
p. cm.
ISBN-13: 978-0-451-22022-6
1. Marriage—Humor. 2. Man-woman relationships—Southern states—Humor. I. Title.
PN6231.M3R55 2007
814'.6—dc22   2006028537

Set in Fournier MT
Designed by Jennifer Ann Daddio

Printed in the United States of America

PUBLISHER'S NOTE
The recipes contained in this book are to be followed exactly as written. The publisher is not responsible for your specific health or allergy needs that may require medical supervision. The publisher is not
responsible for any adverse reactions to the recipes contained in this book.
The publisher does not have any control over and does not assume any responsibility for author or
third-party Web sites or their content.

To Mark, my Southern Yankee,

without whom this would never have been possible.

I love you.

And to Daddy, who lived and died in Dixie.

ACKNOWLEDGMENTS

Writing, I've learned, is a marathon—not a sprint. And I've been at this a good while, which means a whole lot of people have encouraged me, taught me, edited me, prayed for me and just plain blessed me. Without y'all, I would not be where I am today, so all I can say is, I guess I'm going to be baking an awful lot of pecan pie.

First and foremost, I want to thank everyone at New American Library who believed in this book from the beginning and went to bat for it. From the sales and marketing gurus to the graphic designers, publicists, and editorial team, you're the absolute best. Thank you.

I am also immensely grateful for a couple of Yankee Southern Girls. Kim Whalen embraced me, my off-the-wall humor and my literary vision from the get-go, then worked her fanny off to make this book happen. She's an agent *extraordinaire* and I will forever be thankful. And Anne Bohner is a fantastic editor who not only walked me through the publishing process, step by step, but also answered countless questions and was generally more patient than Job as I jiggled a baby on one knee, fielded potty requests and, somehow, amidst it all, wrote this book. For the record, you're both saints—and I'll make sure Mark puts in a good word.

To my Southern Girl author friends: Dottie Benton Frank, whom I could never thank enough for her mentoring, generosity and crazy self—not to mention showing up at my bedside after the arrival of my firstborn; Haywood Smith, for her faith, humor and kindness; Deborah Ford and Ronda Rich, fabulous writers, businesswomen and sweethearts both, who, like all the other gals on this list, hold high the banner of Southern tradition; and of course, Patti Callahan Henry, to whom I will forever be indebted for the introduction to her agent, and whose devotion to family, friends and writing is an inspiration. I am proud to call all y'all friends.

To Tim Bete, for keeping humor alive through the Erma Bombeck Writer's Workshop, and W. Bruce Cameron, one of the funniest men I've ever met. To Bill Star, of the Georgia Center for the Book in Decatur, for supporting writers through the decades, and Charles Connor, of the Harriet Austin Writer's Conference in Athens, who nurtured the dream. To Jackie Cooper and Mike Devine, Southern gentlemen, writers and friends. And to Robin Nelson, Deanna Gomes and Eric Rice, for the gift of their beautiful photos and video, respectively. Thank you all for your support.

To the members of the Ft. Peachtree DAR chapter in Atlanta and the Junior League of DeKalb in Decatur—you're true Southern Girls, and I am proud to know each and every one of you.

And to all the Southern Girls who contributed stories to this book, but who, to Mark's disappointment, shall forever remain nameless so that their husbands, bless their hearts, are not embarrassed. Thank you, from the bottom of my heart.

To all my Southern Girl girlfriends who participated in this book, either directly or indirectly—and who always told me I could: Anita Braaksma, Jasona Brown, Liliana Colgate, Cathy David-Raphoz, Isabelle Droz, Joanna Duke, Louise Dyrenforth-Acker, Teri Easton, Shaunti Feldhahn, Jacinda Holley, Katie Lowry, Emily Lynch, Miranda Natelli, Dana Mercer, Penny Seithel, Lisa Rice, Christine Tucker, Leigh Van Auken, Holland Williams and Annie Wiseman-Floyd. And to Dawn Searcy, my darlin' friend who is always there for me and who filled in the gaps whenever I needed an idea. Y'all are some of the best friends a girl could have.

To Toni and Mardi Dolfo-Smith; Pat and Mike Caven and Peter and Amy Mitchell, who have been great friends during our newlywed years and beyond. To my doctors, nurses and physicians' assistants, for helping us bring our children into the world—especially John Carter, Meera Garcia, Allison Hemingway, Donald Lindblad, Robert Monett and Scott Slayden. To the families of the babysitting coop in Decatur, who helped us keep romance alive after baby number one. And to Erin Murphy and Tawanda Coleman, for taking such great care of that baby while I wrote.

A humongous thank-you to all my "day job" editors, who give my articles a home. To Laura MacCorkle of *Crosswalk*: I cherish your friendship, faith and humor, and I'm proud to be part of the team. To Dianne Bernez and everyone from *Atlanta Woman* magazine, past and present, for supporting books—and me. To Josh Hurst and Tim Porter of *Paste* magazine—you're the bomb, boys. To Jon Rawl, an honest-to-goodness Southern Boy and publisher of *Y'all* magazine. Honey, you've got vision, drive and a super publication. To Courtney Pomeroy and Julie Phillips-Jordon of the award-winning *Athens Banner-Herald*, for the unwavering support and husband stories. And, to Mary Rose Taylor, founder of the Margaret Mitchell House and the Center for Southern Literature, who always told me I should be a journalist. You were right.

To Doris Leigh, publisher of *Southern Flair* magazine, for giving me my first magazine assignment years ago. To Dolly Purvis, former editor of *The Champion* newspaper, where I learned how to be a journalist. And to the many writers and editors I've worked with at the *Atlanta Journal-Constitution*, including Diane Lore, Don O'Briant and Rodney Ho, but especially Valarie Basheda, my dear, dear friend and a fabulous editor. Oh, how I miss the *AJC*— and all of you.

To our mentors, pastors and counselors, especially Marty Barrett; Nicky Gumble; Carol and Murray Moerman; Robb Powell, Doug Rosenau, Steve Stewart and Peter Vaughan. To everyone at All Souls Church in Decatur; Holy Trinity Brompton in London; New Covenant Community in Atlanta; and the Vancouver South Vineyard, for walking the walk with us. And, to the staff and faculty of Regent College in Vancouver, BC, where Mark and I met, married and were infinitely blessed—especially Phil Collins; Gordon Fee; Sharon Forsyth; J. I. "Jim" Packer; Jan and Eugene Peterson; Sven Soderland; Bruce and Elaine Waltke; Rikk Watts and Martha and John Zimmerman.

To Leigh Thornley, Elizabeth Hughes, Linda Benz and Julie Gunn, as well as Patsy Aguirre, Linda Brown, Sharon Egan, Angela Franklin, Peggy Gibson, Denise Gordon, Cheryse Nelson, Molly Raymond, Stephanie Taylor, Sheila White and all the spouses at Vandenberg Air Force Base who have loved us and made us feel so welcome in this strange but wonderful land they call the military.

To my family, for loving me, believing in me and being there whenever I needed you—and for being very, very funny as well as a little bit crazy, which gives me lots of material. I'd especially like to thank Adam, for designing my fabulous Web site, and Bruce, for his time, support and generosity. I still can't believe that Daddy and Ruth are gone, y'all.

Finally, to Mark, my handsome hunk of a holy husband, and my precious girls, Dorothea and Georgia, who take my breath away.

Deo Gloria.
July 2006

CONTENTS

Newlyweds and Marriage: What's Love Got to Do with It?

Marriages are made in heaven.
But, then again, so are thunder, lightning,
tornados and hail.

—UNKNOWN

As my tenth wedding anniversary approached a few years back, I was faced with a mighty big dilemma: did I throw a party—or go hunt for my daddy's shotgun?

Don't get me wrong. I adore my husband. He's hardworking and as honest as your accountant on tax day. He's also funny—especially if you like jokes about obscure biblical characters. Brilliant, too. Don't ask the man to explain something if you're in a hurry. And if all this isn't enough, he's also a looker. Think Tom Cruise, only taller—and no weird religion.

So I'm very proud of being married to him, especially for such a long time. Our conjugal longevity is a real statement in today's love-'em-and-leave-'em world. It's also a family record, of sorts. All four of our parents are on their third marriages, you see. Mark likes to say we don't have a family tree—we have a family briar patch. I prefer to think that we love marriage so much, we do it over and over, despite the risks. Kind of like an extreme sport.

Here's the problem, though. It doesn't matter how sweet or funny or smart or gorgeous your husband is. When you discover your wet beach towels spread out on the oil-stained garage floor—to dry, as my husband explained, like it was the most natural thing in the world—honey, you will not be thinking about his cute little butt. I can tell you that. Heck, one Southern Girl got so scared, she didn't even make it to the altar. Jennifer Wilbanks, Atlanta's infamous Runaway Bride, faked a kidnapping to get out of her wedding. Now maybe it's my imagination, but I think that poor girl must have had a little visit from the bride of Christmas future. I'm telling you—it ain't all Cheerwine and roses.

If you're in the early stages of wedding planning, you'll probably think I'm exaggerating. If you're in the last days (and I do not use the term loosely) of wedding preparation, you'll figure I might have a thing or two to say. If you're on your honeymoon, you're too blissed out to think about anything. But if you're beyond the glorious honeymoon stage—that is, at least four months past your wedding date—you just may think I'm a genius. I'm not, but I am one of the rare ones (with the exception of Dr. Phil, that is) to tell it like it is.

Marriage is one of the greatest inventions on Earth. Married people live longer, are healthier and consistently report greater satisfaction out of life. Of course, they also get more sex, which probably has a lot to do with these findings. But no matter how you look at it, marriage gives us a place to heal and the incentive to grow. When life is good, like a 70-degree, blue-sky afternoon on the front porch, we have somebody to share it with. And when it's bad, like those nights when you've got tears in your ears from crying, there's somebody to hug you. Assuming he isn't freaked out by a woman's tears, that is—which is probably too much to assume at this stage, come to think of it.

I trust in the institution of marriage so much that I don't even advocate living together first. Most people assume that living together makes you more prepared for marriage. Statistics say otherwise—and overwhelmingly so. Couples who live together before marriage are 80 percent more likely to divorce than those who do not. Without a lifelong commitment, it seems, we're far less likely to work through our problems. Then, once we do tie the knot, they come flying at us like a bunch of rusty darts.

I'm no expert, but I've lived with someone and I've married someone else, and I'm convinced that living together is a very bad deal—especially for women. I really hate the old-cow cliché (the one my shocked grandmother used to nag me with during my days of living in sin, long before Mark), but not nearly as much as I hate the fact that she was right. Let's just say that it reminds me of that scene in *Up Close and Personal*, when Michelle Pfeiffer proposes to Robert Redford by telling him that she wants him around every morning.

"But you already have me around in the morning," he says.

"Yes," she replies. "But I want to know you're legally required to be there."

So assuming you've taken the legal plunge—or are about to—how do you prepare for this great commitment? If you're like most people, you don't. The average couple stumbles to the altar after years of free-fall dating, then spends the engagement period preparing for a wedding, not a marriage. But the decision of whether to add a groom's cake to the menu or engrave your invitations doesn't exactly train people to deal with the hurts and dashed expectations that can hit after the honeymoon.

Dating isn't much help, either. There's a lot that I wouldn't want to go back to, when it comes to the so-called olden days, but after years of searching for a decent guy, then bumbling my way through the newlywed period—mostly for lack of example—I long for that time when the most important decision of our lives wasn't made in isolation. I can't help but wonder how much easier it was to meet, date and marry within the context of families, neighbors, communities and churches, rather than bars and singles outings. And, while I have no doubt that some bachelors suffered the unjust scorn of snobby mothers or overprotective dads (as they still do), I'm also sure there were a lot fewer one-night stands when those same suitors were forced to reckon with dear ole dad at the dinner table.

Nowadays, we're lucky if we meet our in-laws prior to the wedding. (Mark and I met ours at the wedding.) With no one to hold us accountable, the whole dating period could be construed as false advertising. I liken it to a season of *The Bachelor*. You walk on the beach at sunset, loll around in the hot tub, dress up for the grand finale, and then, out of all the possible candidates, he picks you! You! You get the rose, the ring, the wedding, the party, and the honeymoon in Fiji. The only problem is, a few months after you get home, your handsome husband has turned into *My Big Fat Fiancé*—without the million dollars in your bank account.

In an ideal world, couples would attend months of premarital counseling with qualified therapists, and they would go before the engagement—not after. After all, who better than professionals to tell us whether to get engaged? Mark and I did, and we've never regretted it. Even though he had already bought the ring when we began our premarital counseling, we decided to postpone the engagement until after we had worked through some of the conflict that counseling had unearthed.

Given the raging popularity of divorce in our families, we knew we needed a lot more help than six or eight discussions about who would be doing the dishes or taking out the trash (him, by the way, on both counts). As Mark said, "In my family, we don't disagree. We divorce." I replied, "In my family, we disagree—loudly, frequently and with flying objects—and then we divorce." Sometimes I think that instead of "Crown Him with Many Crowns" as our wedding processional, they should have played the music from *Psycho*.

Later, of course, we came to realize that most married couples come from families with completely opposite ways of relating. One family will be very vocal and deal with problems head-on, while the other will be prone to silent brooding and ignoring problems. It's like we all have radar and bizarrely gravitate toward our polar opposite. Ever noticed this with your temperature gauges? If you're cold-blooded, you can be sure your spouse will be hot-blooded. During our honeymoon in Hawaii, I would lie on the bed naked,[1] fanning myself and wondering why our condo didn't have air-conditioning. Mark? He was shivering under a winter duvet. I think it's nature's way of having a little fun with us all, in between hurricane season and freak snowstorms in Pascagoula.

So, anyway, to offset some of our risk factors, Mark and I opted for a little disaster planning. Right before the wedding, we signed up for marriage counseling—the real kind. Yep, even though we were madly in love, caught in the throes of prewedding bliss, we tracked down a good counselor.[2] A few weeks after the honeymoon, we went in to deal with our stuff. And, boy, did we have stuff. You'd have thought we were moving to rural Appalachia, we had so much baggage. Suffice to say that when two oldest children marry—especially when one is a Yankee from an all-boy family and the other is a Southerner from an all-girl family—it's like two enemy monarchs trying to share the same palace. Welcome to the Middle Ages.

---

[1]Pronounced "nekkid" by Southerners.
[2]Which, by the way, was as hard to find as a Bloody Mary in a dry county in North Carolina on a wintery Sunday morning.

The real problem with marriage, ya see, isn't how hard it is (although that can certainly be an issue). No, the true challenge is that nobody even hints that marriage is a challenge. Oh, sure, they wink at your wedding and, like late-night comedians, make jokes about it. But nobody comes right out and says that staying married, no matter who you've married, can be a bit like staying at a Motel 6 three blocks from the ocean, when you've been looking forward to a beachfront suite at the Ritz-Carlton all your life. It's hardly the end of the world, it's way better than being at work, but it can be a brutal awakening. And you won't be getting any monogrammed bathrobes.

If only marriage certificates came with warning labels: *Immediately after honeymoon, this man will lose the ability to feed, dress and otherwise take care of himself*. In fact, to clarify things before we get to the point where the woman is even wondering about marriage—meaning, before the second date—I believe that all bachelors should be forced to wear sandwich boards around their necks. This would allow us to make snap decisions about whether to pursue marriage (the second date) by identifying those little habits that make each man so terrifyingly unique.

I drink milk from the jug, frequently scratch my groin and rival my dog for bad breath, one might say. Another would read, *Capable of sitting for seventy-two hours without moving, if television is present (burping included).* My husband's sign would say, *Will always insist on the aisle seat, even when my wife is ten months pregnant and requires seven minutes to squeeze past me.* And what a relief it would be, too. No more nasty surprises. All their sins, laid out like a week-old buffet, for us to select and reject. And say what they may, men would benefit, too. Whenever we complained, they could just turn to us and say, "But, honey, you knew before the second date that I only change my underwear every three days. Why are you so upset?"

Of course, the real reason newlywed brides get so upset is that surprise factor. After all, deciphering the truth about men by asking them to tell you about themselves is a bit like asking a blind man if it looks like rain. This is yet one more reason, by the way, to make sure you meet the most important people in his life: family members, friends and colleagues.[3]

I also believe that brides should be granted permission to make their future mothers-in-law take lie-detector tests—at the expense of the mother-in-law, of course. After all, the blame for most of men's annoying little habits does sit squarely with her. In addition to identifying the truth about your fiancé, no holds barred, it would also establish the parameters of your future relationship with dear old mom: you ask the questions, she answers. While she's hooked up, you might also try a little torture, as a preemptive strike. Say, pulling off one or two of her nail tips right before her Rotary presentation. That way, before she even dreams about commenting on your dusty corners, she'll remember that last-minute, harried trip to the Vietnamese nail salon.

To be fair, the shock of the newlywed year is definitely proportionate to a woman's propensity for denial. Instead of gagging at a boyfriend's nauseating habits, like any respectable married woman would do, many single gals simply write them off as "eccentricities" and assume they can live with them—or worse, change them. It's a recipe for disaster, to be sure. Meanwhile, we married girls are shaking our heads, waiting for the ball to drop.

It's not all uphill, of course. Some things flow as smoothly as the Mississippi. The bedroom, for example—particularly during the early years, when you're getting so much sex your tee-tee[4] will think it's won Lotto South. This, come to think of it, will make the rest of you pretty happy, too. And your husband, well, let's just say that he'll have the biggest cake-eating grin you've

---

[3]But hopefully not ex-girlfriends.
[4]Southern for "vagina."

7

ever seen on his face, every single time you do it, for the next forty years. No news there. Why do you think married men live longer, anyway? Because they're not suffering from Sperm-Retention Syndrome, that's why. Well that, and the fact that they're eating three square meals a day and being forced to go to the doctor whenever the slightest thing ails 'em—unlike women, who tend to cook, clean, go to work and drop off the dry cleaning while suffering from ingrown toenails, migraines and typhoid, all at once.

But the best thing about marriage, when you aren't having sex (which is the overwhelming majority of the time, by the way, after the first year), is the fact that you are far, far away from that jungle where your single friends are cruising the bars, getting their hearts broken by big old apes. It's enough to make you curl up to even the surliest of bad-dog husbands on a rainy night. But you have to get there first, and that takes time—kind of like straightening your hair. It also takes girlfriends. Southern girl-friends.

I wrote this book because, as challenging as my own marriage has been at times, I believe in it more than my dog believes in me. What else are you going to believe in besides undying love in a world that's crazier than a bedbug? If I've learned anything in my decade of conjugal commitment, it's that life can be harder than an unripe peach. It ain't easy, no matter who you are, and we all need somebody beside us to make it all worthwhile.

As with most wives, however, my marital success has not been without its share of headaches, both male- and self-induced. And, oh, how I wish I had known then what I know now. Like how to combat Learned Helplessness in the kitchen, how to make sure a husband remembers your birthday (and gets the perfect gift) and the no-fail method of motivating a man to do housework. I'm even going to tell you how to get your husband to put down the toilet

seat—and much, much more.[5] All this, you see, would have allevi-
ated years of grief for me, as a young bride. I have learned the hard
way that Southern wisdom is worth its weight in boiled peanuts.

Now what I am about to say may not qualify as the be-all and
end-all of marital wisdom. It's certainly not Oprah, but it's not
Jerry Springer, either. Furniture throwing aside (we'll get to that
later), I'm here to tell you that marriage is one of the hardest
things on the planet. I'm not talking about just staying married,
though. Anybody can do that—although hardly anybody does, it
seems. I'm talking about doing it well, and not being miserable.
I'm talking about achieving common goals, with both partners being content, and even joyful.

Those of you who think that marriage will be easy because
you're so in looooooove right now—or because you've never once
had a disagreement—well, just listen up. Creating a successful marriage is one of the toughest things you'll ever do. It's tougher than
uncooked grits. It's tougher than your mother-in-law's heart. It's
even tougher than trying to use the outdoor ladies' room (that is,
the woods) without ruining your new shoes. Of course, when you
finally do it, you'll feel like you've won the Betty Crocker Cook-
off, the Olympic mile and the Congressional Medal of Honor all
on the same day. There is no greater bliss—except the babies
you'll make together, on down the road. But that's a whole 'nother
subject.

Marriage was created to change our lives for the better, and it
does change us, little by little. If you let it, your marriage will make
you more wise, more intuitive and more patient than you've ever
imagined. It will challenge you and mature you. But change does
not come without pain, so be prepared. Be very prepared. No matter how good your marriage is or how wonderful your husband

[5]And I do hope that CNN is standing by, ready for this Breaking News Bulletin.

may be, there will be days when you cannot imagine living with him one more minute. There will be days when you question the moment you walked down that aisle and imagine escape like a would-be Houdini. Someday, you might even eye your daddy's shotgun with too much interest. Trust me, I've been there.

Unfortunately, I can't make marriage any easier.[6] All I can do is make you laugh about it, pass on some hard-won wisdom, and help you see that you're not alone. I don't have all the answers. I have my story—and the stories of other Southern Girls. They are good stories: tragic at times, funny at others. And they have some nuggets to glean, for those who care to sit for a spell. After all, I've managed to stay yoked for more than a decade, and in this day and age (not to mention my family), that is no small thing.

So whether you're unpacking your bags from the honeymoon or heading for that plane back to Memphis, remember that divorce is far worse than anyone is willing to tell you—and most anything you're going through with that husband of yours, too. It's a long, lonely road that may feel like a party at first, but can often be full of flies, blood-sucking mosquitoes and things that go bump in the night—kind of like the Redneck Games in south Georgia. But remember, the evil you know is always better than the evil you don't know. Especially when it comes to men, who can be some of the most evil things on the planet, bless their sexy little hearts.

One thing is certain, though. You married the man, so there must be a whole lot of good in there somewhere. So chin up and keep reading. And remember, if all else fails, there's always Daddy's shotgun.

---

[6]And if I could, I'd be a surefire winner of the next Nobel peace prize.

ONE

Southern Girls Revisited: The Devil Went Down to Georgia

Once upon a time, there was a place called the South. It was a wonderful land, full of breathtaking scenery, balmy weather and tacky lawn ornaments. The people who inhabited this land were called Southerners, and they were friendly and gracious. Southerners enjoyed spending time together, especially if it involved eating or football. They did things slowly, and understood that faith, family, honor and tradition—along with a good redneck joke—were the foundations of a life well lived.

Far away from the South was another, very different place called the North. The North was a cold place, where people talked very quickly. Yankees, as the North's inhabitants were called, liked to rush around. They had a good baseball team, went to the theater a lot and knew how to hail cabs. And their pizza and bagels were excellent, but the Yankees had no time to enjoy them.

After many years of mocking the South, the Yankees began to hear rumors about its wonders. One day, a small group went to visit. To their amazement, the South was even more wonderful than they had heard. It had beaches, mountains, plains and marshes. It had cheap waterfront property. And although the Southerners couldn't understand a word the Yankees said and wore brightly colored clothes, they were kind, and fried chicken for the Yankees.

The Yankees loved the South. They could swim in her waters. They could eat pecan pie. They could buy beach houses. So the Yankees began to move. The first ones to come were old—very old. They came in RVs and went straight to Florida, which soon lost its Southern status. But younger Yankees came, too. They moved to Southern cities, where they set up restaurants, served unsweet tea and refused to yield to oncoming traffic. Before long, in the wake of Yankee influence, Southerners were forgetting to use turn signals and RSVP to parties. They said "you guys." They even stopped writing thank-you notes.

Meanwhile, in a place called Hollywood, screenwriters who had never set foot in the South were writing about it. Producers and directors who confused Hoppin' John with Johns Hopkins were making movies about Southern ways. Actors who couldn't tell a Carolina lilt from a Kentucky twang were portraying Southerners. And people all over the world thought Southerners were ignorant hicks.

So one day, a group of women decided they'd had enough. They would take back the South and reinvent it. They would entertain and socialize across ethnic and racial divides. They would have successful careers and volunteer. They would cook, clean and have happy families. And they would RSVP and write thank-you notes.

The South had risen again. The Southern Girl had been reborn.

Rebel, Rebel

I don't know about you, but am I the only one who's had it up to here with the caricatures? I swannee, if you listen to Hollywood, Southerners are either wannabe Scarletts, alcoholic preachers or gun-totin' rednecks. Not only that, but we're all morons, too—and about as backward as a pickup packed with day laborers. So I think it's high time somebody set the record straight. As one of my relatives said, "I can assure you that not all Southerners are from Tobacco Road."

Indeed.

Now there are definitely rednecks in the South, no doubt about that. But, as far and as wide as my travels have taken me, I have yet to hear anyone use that bizarre, made-up, nineteenth-century Charleston accent that non-Southern actors always adopt, thinking they're being so authentic. Not only that, but despite a solid history of award-winning Southern writers—many of whom happen to be among the living—clueless non-Southern screenwriters still portray the average Southerner using generalizations, absurd dialogue and every cliché imaginable. Cinematic Scarletts dress up to go to the Piggly-Wiggly, wear Grandmother's pearls to weed the hydrangeas and rue the day that the Junior League opened up membership. Their male counterparts aren't much better. All they do is burn crosses, booze it up and rape their daughters—and that's just the preachers. It's enough to make Stonewall Jackson gallop in front of enemy lines again.

Now rednecks, it must be said, are their own ball of wax, and frankly, it's impossible to caricature them because they are walkin', talkin', gawkin' clichés. In other words, we make fun of them, too. Redneck women think "fashion" is a right-wing political party. They wear big hair, too much makeup, and faded jeans that are way too small—usually with rhinestone belts. They've made an art of cooking slimy things called okra and bottom suckers called catfish (although the rest of us love those dishes, too). They think Wal-Mart is high style, barbecue is fine dining, macaroni-and-cheese is a vegetable and every story in *The National Enquirer* is gospel truth.

When it comes to redneck men, comedian Jeff Foxworthy's the expert. According to him, a redneck man will use the same tree as his hunting dog. He'll keep a can of Raid on the kitchen table and entertain himself for hours with a fly swatter. He has the local taxidermist on speed dial, thinks *The Nutcracker* is something you do off the high dive, and Lord help him if his front porch ever collapses, because it will kill at least six dogs.

If you're like most Southerners, you have at least one redneck (also known as trailer trash) in your clan—no matter how many country clubs you belong to. Up North, he's known as the family blacksheep. Down here, he's the family redneck. Unfortunately, we have several in my family, but we inherited most through marriage—which is one of the major downsides to that otherwise glorious institution. The worst one is a distant relative, but he couldn't be more embarrassing if he tried. Actually, I think he is trying. He lives with his elderly mama and is chain-smoking himself to death in front of the TV, waiting for her to die. When she goes, he'll be a wealthy man. But only for about six months, until he spends it all. In the meantime, he's as surly as a snake in a woodpile, and I'm just waiting for my brother to take Daddy's advice and cuss his butt out, as he swears he will someday. Cussing somebody out, by the way, is a Southern art form.

Most Southern women (and men) fall somewhere between the stereotypes. We might be from the country, where we raise chickens, enjoy the fresh air and tend to our 'maters.[7] Or we might be

---

[7]Tomatoes.

from the growing number of Southerners who make the city our home, with busy careers, condos and commutes. No matter where we live, however, our identity is firmly rooted in family and up-bringing. From the time we can speak, our mamas train us to re-spect strangers, those in authority and our elders (anyone more than a day older than us) by saying "Yes, Ma'am" and "Yes, Sir." They teach us to eat everything on our plate, so as not to offend, along with all the manners we need to sail through any social situation—and then some. They tell us what to wear and what not to wear (especially before and after Labor Day). Pink and green on a man? Not a problem. Pastels are our primary color palette. And finally, our mamas encourage us not to be "ugly," or impo-lite, by using a host of euphemisms like "Bless her heart" and "Isn't that sweet?", which make us sound like we're being sweet when we're actually being ugly.

Growing up, our daddies insisted that boys respect us, then showed us how to respect our alma maters—by purchasing season tickets. They also taught us that there isn't a man good enough for us on the planet Earth, which has been known to cause more than a few problems when choosing a mate. And, in between drilling us in the art of Southern hospitality, which kicks into high gear dur-ing all major holidays and a few obscure ones as well, our grand-mothers taught us how to get away with murder (sometimes, quite literally), by smiling wide enough.

As a result, most of us would rather lose an Hermès scarf than forget to write a thank-you note—and we still obsess about that one time we did forget. We feel guilty that men always pick up the dinner tab, but are greatly relieved that they do. We have at least one crazy relative (not including Mother) in the family.

We don't really like mint juleps, except maybe on Kentucky Derby Day, but we can sure make a mean margarita. We can't go a day without sweet tea, however. We own pearls that we frequently feel compelled to wear. We host showers when friends get married, with silver that's been in the family for generations (but which, tragically, we cannot afford to add to). And for funerals, we always bring a dish that is baked from scratch (by the grocery store, that is).

We celebrate Martin Luther King Day and eat king cake for Mardi Gras. We hold Super Bowl cookouts, St. Patrick's Day parties, Fourth of July picnics, and holiday open houses. We volunteer at soup kitchens, boys and girls clubs and with the Junior League—a very modern, multiracial and hardworking Junior League, not your mother's Junior League. We subscribe to *Southern Living*. We go to church or synagogue. We tithe. We donate to charity. And we're all in therapy.

Top Ten Signs You're a Southern Woman

- You are mysteriously drawn toward pink and green.
- You obsess over thank-you notes.
- You own a set of pearls and feel compelled to wear them. Frequently.
- You have a pitcher of sweet tea on your kitchen counter.
- You have at least one crazy relative and one redneck in your family.
- You say "Yes, ma'am" and "Yes, sir" to strangers, those in authority and anyone who looks a day older than you.
- You subscribe to *Southern Living*.
- You volunteer and entertain religiously.
- You attend church or synagogue.
- You are (or need to be) in therapy.

Say You, Say Me

Southerners have a very special way of speaking. It isn't just our accents—which, by the way, are as diverse as our topography. It's our expressions, too. "Well, butter my butt and call me a biscuit," my godmother is fond of saying. In a South Carolina restaurant, I once heard someone mutter, "My cow died last night, so I don't need your bull." My maternal grandfather had a host of expressions that he'd use from his front porch in Belzoni, Mississippi. "It's been hotter'n a goat's butt in a pepper patch," he'd say. But my favorite was "The higher the monkey climbs the pole, the more he shows his tail." Except Papa didn't say "tail," if you know what I mean.

Even if you stripped away the accent and the picturesque expressions, you'd still recognize Southern speech. When I came back to the South after living abroad for a decade, I had forgotten how very much Southerners love to talk about one another—until my best friend started telling me the life story of every human she met at the grocery store. When traveling through a small town, try asking a Southern man for directions. He'll describe the history of every building, street and shrub on your way, offer several different routes[8] (one highway, one through town), then finally give up and tell you to just follow him, 'cause he's going that direction anyhow.

A Southern woman will exclaim that her aunt's second cousin went to that school over there, then spend five minutes trying to figure out who she knows that you might know. She'll tell you all about the murder trial that just took place in the courthouse, the reporter who made everyone mad and how so-and-so's wife left him 'cause he spent so much time at the trial. She won't remember

---

[8]Rhymes with "out," if you're Southern—not "roots."

any of the street names, but she'll give you a great landmark: that big ole tree that looks like a car hit it, but didn't; it just grew that way. Ten minutes later, you'll be on your way.

For some strange reason, outsiders call this "gossip," and they can grow mighty impatient when we ramble on and spin our yarns. We don't really understand this. After all, what's the point of life if you can't take a minute or two to enjoy it? There's no way around it, though. If somebody cuts us off, we'll just get flustered and start all over again. Then we'll talk about them.

Another hallmark of Southern communication is the "prayer request"—again, not to be confused with gossip. To illustrate, a relative once sent me the following e-mail:[9]

> Please pray for my life-long friend Betsy, who lives in Augusta but is from Charlotte and went to boarding school with me in Memphis. We were majorettes together and she was president of the debate club in high school. Her precious son, Steven, who is an attorney in Savannah, is married to an awful woman who must weigh 300 pounds, bless her heart, and smokes pot. She doesn't bathe or feed the children. They are 4 and 7 and the sweetest children you have ever met—all due to Steven, of course. He has just had surgery for a brain tumor. They couldn't get it all and he must now undergo a series of radiation treatments.
>
> Betsy's life has been full of tragedy. Her mother was killed by a drunk driver when she was sixteen, right before majorette tryouts. (She made the team anyway.) Her father, who had been having an affair, broke up with that mistress and married a woman that he met at the funeral, of all places. Betsy's new stepmother made her life miserable— and her father would never do anything about it. Betsy's

---

[9]The names and places have been changed to protect the insane.

daughter, Courtney, died tragically as a child. My mother said she had never seen a more beautiful or sweeter child than Courtney (I was living in Winston Salem at the time—this was before my divorce from Bill). After that, Betsy and her husband divorced. She had another son, years later (he now lives in Durham and works for the railroad) but the father of the boy died before he and Betsy could get married.

The stepmother finally died this year, but totally cut Betsy out of the will. Now, not only will Betsy not get a dime from her family home OR the beach house at Hilton Head—which they had bought with the money from her mother's insurance policy, I might add—but Betsy's not even allowed to go into the house to get any of that beautiful furniture that was handed down to her mother from her grandmother. Betsy's mother and my mother were very close. She was a wonderful woman, born in Newnan, who used to make the best strawberry pie. Her furniture is very old and quite magnificent—some pieces date back to Revolutionary times. It just makes me weep.

So please remember to pray for Steven's radiation treatments. And feel free to pass this email along so that other people will, too.

Did you keep any of this straight? Congratulations. You must be Southern. Otherwise, here's a recipe that might come in handy:

Southern Sweet Tea

As any true Southerner knows, there's no excuse for fake tea. "Sweet" is one thing—and we think that's the only way to go.

But if you really want to disgust a Southern Girl, just hand over a glass of the stuff that comes out of some dispenser. Thankfully, Southern Sweet Tea is easy and quick to make. This lasts about a day, if people don't drink it all first.

1. Fill a saucepan with cold water.
2. Bring to a roiling boil (with lots of bubbles).
3. Add 2 or 3 family-sized tea bags (I prefer Luzianne) and remove from heat.
4. Add a cup or so of sugar and let steep for at least twenty minutes. More is better.
5. Pour into a pitcher and add cold water to taste.
6. Serve over ice, with a slice of lemon, in a pretty glass— or maybe an old mason jar (very Southern). For a treat, substitute a mint sprig for the lemon.
7. Keep the pitcher of tea on the counter—not in the fridge.

Something in the Way She Moves

This is a book about Southern Girls, however—not Southerners. And while the two concepts do overlap, it is important to note that they are also quite distinct. First, however, you may be asking why I have chosen to use the term "Southern Girl." Why not "woman?" Why not "lady?" Why not "belle?"

Well, if you are a Southern Girl, I need not say another word. You know who you are—and who you are not. But for the uninitiated, allow me to explain.

"Belle," being the French word for "beautiful," is, of course, applicable at all times to Southern women. We are natural-born beauties, and we work very hard and spend lots of money to stay that way. But the term is slightly overused nowadays, don't you think? And perhaps just a tad misleading as well. That expression has been used for generations to describe the daughters of the Confederacy, and we don't want anyone to get confused and think "hoopskirts." We're also trying to broaden our horizons here. After all, being a true Southern Girl has little to do with being born in or living in a certain area of the country. And it's certainly not about the color of your skin.

As for "lady," that goes without saying. We are all ladies. At least that's what our mothers told us, and God knows they're never wrong about anything. But that title, unlike other titles— such as Mardi Gras queen, homecoming queen or Lompoc Flower Festival queen, which were created to be thrown in people's faces—is not something you toss around. It is something that comes from years of faithfully writing those thank-you notes, making (or buying) that funeral food and volunteering your fanny[10] off. It's valuable, even though some people just don't appreciate it anymore. Bless their hearts.

Some may ask about the term "girls," as opposed to "women," but Southerners understand one very important fact, and that is that females from the South never grow old. Any Southern boy who enjoys life as we know it on this green Earth would never dream of mentioning the word "age" to a Southern Girl, and certainly not with a questioning lilt to his voice. If you don't believe me, ask anyone in my family what happened when one of the children questioned my grandmother about her age. Let's just say that Taffy, her teeth-baring, toddler-eating bloodhound Chihuahua had nothing on dear Marmee, and leave it at that. My own mother,

[10]Southern for "bottom," "read end" or "butt."

who's in so much denial about being a grandmother that she insists our kids call her "Auntie Kay," sometimes claims she's my older sister. With a straight face. "You know you're really getting old," she always says, "when you start lying about your children's ages." I guess so.

So, extreme measures (and makeovers) notwithstanding, Southern women simply do not age. We used to be little girls. Now we're big girls, and that's all there is to it.

Finally, I must point out—and however tragic it may be—that just as some Western and even Northern girls are actually true Southern Girls in heart and spirit, not every "southern girl" is a Southern Girl. There are southern girls, and there are Southern Girls—and a world of difference stretches between the two.

Southern girls just happen to have been born south of the Mason-Dixon Line, and maybe even raised there, but they only think they are true Southern Girls. Sadly, those southern girls do not have the charisma, breeding or anything that might remotely resemble the charm of a true Southern Girl—much less the skeletons in the family closet. These southern girls have never considered volunteering in a homeless shelter, don't donate to charity and think "goodwill" is something you feel on Christmas Eve. They are racist. They don't understand manners—which were created to make people feel honored and at ease, and not for any kind of social snobbery. Moreover, these girls have probably never written a thank-you note in their lives. But the greatest crime by far of pseudo-southern girls, bless their tacky, withered little hearts, is that they do not understand friendship.

So what does it mean to be a Southern Girl? Two words: respect and loyalty.

Angel of the Morning

A true Southern Girl understands and practices respect. No matter how rushed she may be, she will greet her bus driver by name, compliment her cashier and ask about the custodian's kids. She may disagree with the way her in-laws handle finances, but she'll keep her thoughts to herself (and a few select friends, of course). She frequently says "Yes, Ma'am" and "Yes, Sir," like her mother taught her. She tips well, shows up for important events and re-members birthdays (however belatedly at times). And she always shakes hands and compliments her opponent after a sporting match—especially if she's just lost.

Southern Girls loathe the thought of being rude, tacky or in-appropriate, so a true Southern Girl wouldn't dream of writing a tell-all book about her lovers, no matter how famous they might be. Kissing another woman at a nationally televised awards cere-mony? Too tacky for words. And showing one of her ta-tas,[11] like Janet Jackson at the Super Bowl? Honey, perish the thought. You don't see Faith Hill doing that sort of thing, now do you?

A true Southern Girl is also loyal. She may not be perfect (well, okay, pretty darn close), but she'd walk barefoot on summer sand be-fore she'd let anyone talk ugly about her friends. And if that husband of yours ever hurts your feelings, she's there. A Southern Girl would never have taped poor Monica Lewinsky, for example much less turned her in. But a Southern Girl would have also warned Hillary about Bill—long before she married him. Same thing for Lisa-Marie and Michael Jackson. (What was she thinking?) A Southern Girl would never have let Martha Stewart get too big for her britches—much less build an elevator for her car. But a Southern Girl would

---

[11]Southern for "breasts."

have been right there beside her on the witness stand, denying it all, then bringing her lipstick at the prison.

A true Southern Girl would have assured Jennifer Lopez, again and again, that it was not her fault it didn't work out with all those men. She would have never even hinted that Starr Jones was fat—but she certainly would have chipped in for that surgery. She would not, however, have told Pamela Lee Anderson to get rid of the silicone. Big boobs are still a bit hit in the South. Alas, the bigger the better—as Pam finally realized.

The truth is, it doesn't matter where a Southern Girl was born; it's the character that counts. Do you love your neighbor more than the buttered side of toast loves the floor, yet still insist on a makeover? Would you let your roots grow out, rather than repeat malicious gossip? Would you carry a baby for your friend, even if it meant another three years at Weight Watchers? Answer yes to any of these questions, and you're probably a Southern Girl—and don't let any Yankee tell you differently.

Let's Hear It for the Boy

As a Southern Girl, you may or may not be married to a Southern Boy. I personally married a Yankee, and while I have no intention of giving him up, it's not something I can strongly recommend.[12] After years of living in Europe, where I attended college and grad school, I thought that my Southern tendencies were buried. But marriage, as you are about to see, has a way of digging things up.

Southern Boys (that's what we call 'em, even if they use a walker, and I personally think it's a very accurate term) may be hard to typify, but they have very easily recognizable characteristics. The

---

[12]Unless he's Nicolas Cage, of course.

gentleman Southern Boy (which should be redundant, and refers to Southern Boys who were raised right by their mamas) will always open a lady's door, pay for her dinner and give her his jacket when it gets cold (as in, below 70 degrees Fahrenheit). He won't cuss in front of her, save the occasional slipup, and will always rise when she enters the room. He'll treat his pregnant wife like a mythical goddess, and he'll say her name with the sweetest accent you've ever heard, dragging two syllables out to five and five to ten. And if you think that sounds corny or country, then stick around when one pronounces mine. It'll make you swoon.

Just like any God-fearing redneck, however, the true Southern Boy will dream of owning a "pick-'em-up" truck. We do not know why this is, especially when the only thing he needs to haul is a set of golf clubs on Saturday morning. Maybe he thinks it matches the ball caps he so loves to wear, but the truck is sine qua non for a Southern Boy. He may have a garage full of SUVs and Mercedes, but he'll give that truck a name (Lucille, Ruby, and Black Pearl come to mind) and park it right next to his other vehicles—including the Harley. And he may not hang a gun rack in the back window, but you can be sure he wishes he could.

They're an interesting lot, Southern Boys, and though far from perfect, are about as close as that sex can get to flawlessness. I personally believe that Adam, the only sinless man to ever grace this planet, was a Southern Boy. And speaking of Adam, I need to set something straight.

I Heard It Through the Grapevine

Although every preacher I've ever heard likes to tell it this way, it was not Eve's fault that she and Adam got kicked out of the Garden of Eden. I'm not saying she was sinless perfection or anything, but if you read the Genesis story closely, you'll notice that when Eve speaks to the snake, she gives him wrong information. She naively informs the creature that God forbid them to eat from "the tree in the middle of the garden." She further tells him that they are not even allowed to touch that tree.

Well, first of all, there were two trees—not one—in the middle of the garden: the tree of life and the tree of knowledge of good and evil. The fact that Eve only mentioned one tree, therefore, probably means that she had never even been to the middle of the garden. If she had, she certainly hadn't spent much time there, because she didn't notice the all-important tree of life, which had to be pretty big. To make matters worse, poor old Eve thought they would die if they even touched "the tree."

The problem, of course, is that all God ever said was not to eat from the tree of knowledge of good and evil. They were completely free to eat from the other tree. In fact, we can safely assume that Adam, who knew this, was indeed partaking. So how did Eve get so mixed up—and so deprived? Especially since sweet little Eve wasn't even created when God laid down the law. In my ex-lawyer opinion, the evidence points straight to Adam—who got his info directly from the top. But why, you ask, would a loving husband give his wife wrong information about something as important as food, especially when the wife was the one turning it into homemade fruit pies for his little sneaky self?

I see two possibilities. One, Adam was hogging the middle of the garden. He misled Eve so he would have a secret place to hang out and watch football, without being nagged to mow the lawn. It was, after all, a very big lawn. Two, Adam simply couldn't take down a decent message. It certainly wouldn't be the first time. Well, actually, it would be. The very first time, in fact. Which may explain why every man since Adam has been embedded with his defective message-taking gene.

Ah, but the inability to take down messages is only one annoying habit that will plague you from your husband's side of the world. Southern Boys, in particular, have an entire repertoire of ways to drive us crazy, not the least of which is their expectation that we take care of the most mundane duties in life while doing everything else, as well. A story is told about a recent flight from Chicago to Houston. The plane was passing through a severe storm and the turbulence was awful. Things went from bad to worse when one of the wings was struck by lightning.

A female passenger at the front of the plane became very agitated and stood up. "I'm too young to die!" she wailed. "But if I have to, I want my last minutes on Earth to be memorable! Is there anyone on this plane who can make me feel like a woman, right here and now?"

Silence. Then suddenly, from the rear of the plane, a handsome Texan stood. He had curly brown hair and big blue eyes, and as he walked toward the woman, he smiled and slowly began removing his shirt. One by one, the buttons came undone, until he stood before her bare-chested, his muscles rippling. He reached for her. She gasped. Then she heard him whisper, "Here, honey. Iron this and get me something to eat."

Oh, despite their charms, it's hard not to wonder if Southern Boys just might be the very reason why the divorce rate is skyrocketing around this country. It certainly is the reason behind the Southern divorce rate, and Southern men have been known to migrate. After all, though wonderful as far as men go, Southern Boys are still men. So who's a Southern Girl to give advice on anything, much less an institution that is crumbling before our very eyes?

May I respectfully suggest that it is precisely this reason—that is, the sheer impossibility of successful marriage to any man without a miracle from the Lord God On High—that Southern Girls are actually the ones best suited to giving marital advice. In fact, we do this all the time. It's one of the things that makes us Southern Girls. That, and talking in general.

But the real reason a Southern Girl is qualified to give advice—regardless of who she married—is that she has true marital credentials. And those credentials, as I have been able to ascertain, while certainly limitless, can be summarized as follows: patience, perseverance, persecution and the ability to withstand great suffering.

Marriage, above all else, requires patience. And what Southern Girl does not have patience? After all, we waited all that time for our men to marry us, didn't we? Southern Girls also understand perseverance. We know what it's like to sit through never-ending sermons wearing stockings and high heels in 95-degree heat and 100 percent humidity, because the deacons haven't fixed the doggone air-conditioning. We definitely understand persecution. We have Southern mothers. And finally, we understand suffering. How else can you account for the 49 percent of marriages that do not end in divorce?

So the fact of the matter is, under their perplexing, multifaceted exteriors, Southern Girls have a lot going for them. A whole lot. And if you want to believe all those clichés about us, go right ahead. But be forewarned. While you are snickering away, a Southern Girl just might be tearing you to pieces on the tennis court—or in the courtroom. Remember steel magnolias? They coined the term for us, honey. We may look soft and smell sweet but inside, we are tougher than our acrylic nails. And we scratch, too. Which means we are infinitely qualified to give advice about men.

So, darlin', when it comes to men and marriage, thou shalt not fear. The Southern Girl is here. And this Southern Girl, like most Southern Girls, is never short on advice—especially in the relationship department. So pour yourself some sweet tea, pull up a chair and turn on the fan, hon. We got something to talk about.

TWO

Picking a Place to Live:
The Love Shack

According to the nineteenth-century poet and author Oliver Wendell Holmes, "Where we love is home." But, like the many things which are about to be redefined by your new union, this decision shall put a whole new twist on the old question of "your place or mine."

House of Pain

Many years ago, a sweet Labrador retriever named Huntley used to walk his mistress in the same park where my mother's dogs walked her. Now Huntley was not the sort of dog to intentionally mark every square inch that he passed on his daily outings. Had he been a younger dog, and fully in control of his bladder, Huntley would have simply squirted here and there, here and there, as he skipped around the park taking care of business. Those places, few and far between, would have been Huntley's territory.

When we made Huntley's acquaintance, however, he was rather advanced in age and had lost control of this all-important doggy function. He also waddled instead of walked. This meant that dear, sweet Huntley made a terrible mess everywhere he went. After he had sprayed, he kept on spraying. And spraying. And spraying. As he walked along the path, Huntley's you-know-what would sway left and right, letting forth a steady stream of pee[13] that soaked everything in sight. Huntley didn't realize what was happening, bless his little dog heart. But that didn't stop him from thinking that he owned every square inch of that park, either. Whenever he arrived, he took one whiff—no matter where he happened to be standing—and he was master of his domain. Top dog. King of the world. Because he had marked it.

I tell you this story not to point out that men will get old and lose control of their bladders. They will, but so will we, and the only thing we can do about that is pray that the landfills will somehow keep up with all the adult diapers threatening to overtake the planet. The point of my Huntley story is that men are like Huntley— and the older they are, the worse they become.

You see, Huntley never intended to become a fountain of urine, marking the world's playground as his private castle. He was just out for a good time, hoping to let people know he was still in the game. But the older he got, the more control he lost. He marked and marked, until there was nothing left to mark. Most of

[13]Although the word "tee-tee" is frequently used as both a verb and noun by Southern Girls, to describe both the female organ and the specimen springing forth from that organ, when referring to the urine of an animal, a Southern Girl will almost always substitute the word "pee."

the time, Huntley didn't even know he was spraying, but spray he did, with alarming frequency, wherever and whenever he could.

When it comes to their homes (and I use the word loosely), men have a tendency to behave exactly like Huntley. Like dogs bred in captivity, they can be very cute—and very welcome on cold winter nights. But they are incontinent markers, and woe to the woman who tries to move in on their territory. I learned this the hard way when I tried to use my new husband's office supplies. In my family, we shared everything, so it was only natural (or I assumed) for me to borrow whatever I wanted from Mark. In fact, since we were married, I didn't even see it as "borrowing." He did, however, and that's putting it mildly.

Mark insists the problem was not that I used his things, but that I didn't return them immediately. And, I confess, sometimes I did allow a few hours to pass before putting back those possessions. On the other hand, Mark also seems to have a tiny issue with sharing. To solve the scissors "problem," for example, he went out and bought a dozen pair. We now have scissors in every room of the house. You can even go to the bathroom chez Robertson and clip coupons, if you want, because the scissors are within reach.

Surprisingly, a man's kitchen is an area that is fraught with "marked" territory. If your new husband is like most men, for example, he will not understand why he needs more than one pot. After all, men don't cook. They heat. His lone pot, which he occasionally uses on the stove (out of deference to his mother, who taught him to do this before microwaves became de rigueur), will likely be covered in so much grime that putting food into it would be tantamount to eating raw chicken left under the Florida sun. Just like your grandmother's cast-iron frying pan, you see, men season their pots. Trying to convince him you need new ones, therefore, will be impossible.

Also, just because he uses the microwave does not mean he will have a decent one. If he's like most men, his will date back to the early eighties and will be a horrendous shade of poop brown—which may just match his kitchen floor. But there's no need to buy a new one, so don't even ask. It works fine.

During graduate school, a girlfriend and I rented a multistory house with four guys. We were feeling a little insane at the time, being single and all, and thought it would be fun. Plus, we figured they would introduce us to their friends. We moved out three weeks later after walking in on them, in the living room, trying to blow out a candle—from behind. Four gorgeous, successful men in their mid- to late twenties, holding a wind contest. Talk about a reality check.

Prior to that little revelation, I happened to see them in the kitchen one night. They were lined up, waiting to use the one pot they collectively "owned." One after the other, these boys cooked their food, washed the pot, then handed it over to the next guy. Meanwhile, they chatted and drank beer, as if they had all the time in the world.

The most amazing thing about this scenario was that even though one of them was cooking spaghetti—which, call me Julia Child, but in my household would necessitate two pots, even with a jar of Ragu—their "system" still prevailed. Not only that, but they acted confused when I suggested they buy more pots—say, at a garage sale, like the one where they'd purchased the first one.

"Why?" one said. "It would just make more mess."

"But don't you get tired of waiting?"

They looked as if I'd suggested they check out the final score of a ballgame they'd TiVoed.

"What about eating together?" I insisted. "Don't you ever want to do that?"

One shrugged. "We don't have time," he said.

*Exhaustive Inventory of
the Single Man's Kitchen*

- Old, seasoned pot
- Frying pan—with or without handle
- Harvest Gold blender from 1972
- Combination bottle opener and corkscrew
- Can opener
- Pizza cutter
- 342 plastic plates, take-out cups and water bottles

In addition to one lonely pot, a man's kitchen will typically contain an ancient frying pan with a handle that is about to fall off, a Harvest Gold–colored blender (for protein shakes), a combination bottle opener and corkscrew, a can opener, a pizza cutter, plates of varying patterns and two shelves of plastic take-out cups and water bottles. He will not own a dishwasher. His air-conditioning will only work sporadically. But never fear, because his dog, who just loves to chew on your Jimmy Choos, will always have working equipment, necessitating regular walks and a lifetime supply of Formula 409.

He will have ugly furniture—very ugly furniture—but he will not realize this. He may sleep on a water bed—something that men seem to think is sexy, rather than what it actually is: a breeding ground for Ebola. The electronic factor will also be significant, and he will likely have a major investment (far more than his 401[k] or IRA) poured into all sorts of equipment you've never even heard of, unless you happen to move in techie circles. We're talking tens of thousands, if not more. Despite their value, however, these items will be sitting on cinder blocks and plastic milk crates. My husband still loves this kind of "furniture," and gets really excited whenever the U.S. Postal Service delivers our mail in one of their little plastic bins, after a vacation. He has so many, all he needs is the little outfit to impersonate a mailman.

What few pieces of furniture your husband does have—say, a sofa and a recliner, the former in orange velour, the latter in fake leather dating from the sixties or seventies—will be arranged in a semicircle, in the center of the room, facing his electronic idols. My father-in-law, who has been married for almost twenty years to his current wife, lives and works in another city. On weekends, he commutes to her house, four hours away. But during the week, he lives like a bachelor. He has a total of three pieces of furniture in his apartment: a bed, a nightstand and a leather recliner facing a plasma television.[14]

If you move into your husband's home, he will not understand why you don't appreciate weights in the dining room. After all, he works out every day, whereas you entertain only once or twice a month, at best. But weights will be the least of your worries, because if he is like most men, his home will be completely filled with sports equipment. Some, like his hockey sticks and skis, will serve as reminders of the glory days. Other items, like his basketball and soccer cleats, exist for inspiration. The rest will be used for fake sports, like pool and poker.

Art will be sports- or female-related. With a bit of persuasion, he might comprehend why you do not want a poster of Troy Aiken or Beyoncé in the living room. However, unless he is a midget, he will insist on placing the pictures that you do agree on, football-inspired or not, far too high on the walls. My husband, who is six-one, believes that the perfect height for paintings (which he happens

---

[14]At least the chair is made out of real leather.

to define as portraits of General Lee) is five feet, eleven inches from the ground. He calls this "eye level."

Advantages of Moving into His Place

- Big TV
- Good stereo
- Home gym in living room
- No use vacuuming
- No need for yellow pages (just read plastic cup collection)

Men often put their creativity to work when it comes to displaying items like hot-sauce collections and beer containers. Shelving created from two-by-fours or milk cartons is popular. Handfuls of peanut shells may be scattered around the room in eclectic groupings. But no matter how much you complain, he will refuse to move these items (except for, perhaps, the peanuts). It's his place, and he likes it this way. *Comprende?*

The three towels he owns, which barely wrap around your head (much less your waist), bear the logos of motels frequented by the local crack-ho contingent. His only set of sheets does not match. And then there are all those interesting items that he and only he could dream of buying. My sister, God bless her, had to put up with a puffy black toilet seat. After she moved into her husband's place (see what that gets you?), he just plain refused to remove it, no matter how much she protested. He also had black leather sofas, but they were nothing compared to the toilet seat. I can only imagine the humiliation.

Mark and I had our fair share of fights over the decorative toilet seat cover—the fuzzy one that matched our blue bath mat, back when seat covers were still popular. For years, he would take it off and hide it, until I finally relented. (It had gone out of style by then, anyway). However, as far as I'm concerned, puffy black toilet seats would have been a deal breaker. You have to choose your battles, though, and fortunately, my sister's husband is far more wonderful than his decorating tastes are questionable.

The biggest problem with moving into a man's place is not just how ugly his things are, however—it's getting rid of them, which can be more difficult than a cat covering poop on a marble floor. First of all, the longer he's been single, the more entrenched these habits will be. And God forbid that any members of his family have donated these items, in which case you should run, not walk, from the idea of moving in. Because as soon as you touch that item, you will be tampering with his childhood—perhaps even his mother's taste. And any Southern Girl knows you don't mess with Southern Mothers.

Second, your primary means of getting rid of his stuff is called "losing it during the move." But if you move in with him, that option is forever lost. Even if certain items just happen to "disappear," he'll notice. God knows how my stepmother put up with all the ammunition my father had in their home. Not only did it fill several dressers and closets around the house; it was also scattered like loose change in unexpected places. You never knew when you might open a drawer and see a handful of bullets come flying at you. And I won't even go into Daddy's gun collection— or the decades-old stacks of gun and hunting magazines.

Other possessions may appear to be innocuous, but haunt you nonetheless. For six years, I was awakened by the most painful noise at five thirty a.m. My husband called it his alarm clock, but its honking was so loud it summoned every goose within a hundred miles. I begged and pleaded for Mark to replace the thing, which also kept me awake at night with its bright red light. Finally, in a state of severe sleep deprivation, I lost it. I took a hammer to that clock and sent it back to Tick-Tock Heaven.

To this day, my husband swears that I destroyed something of great sentimental value. He enjoys telling those who might be shocked how demon possessed I became with that clock. And this, I admit, can be slightly embarrassing. However, Mark now makes sure to consult me when buying items that interrupt my sleep at ungodly hours. And, while I still have to hit him in the arm every morning at five thirty when his (new) alarm clock goes off, it's just a soft digital beep. Sometimes, he even hides it under the pillow for his multiple snoozes. It's all in the training, girls.

Other reasons for not moving into his place include the fact that you don't get along with his neighbors—the drunk transvestites milling outside his bedroom window at four in the morning, for example. You want walls with color, but his are all white—and he insists he likes them that way. You don't appreciate shag carpeting, with or without the wine stains. And, weights or no weights, his place simply has no room to entertain.

So this, dear Southern Girl, is your escape hatch. His place is just too small for you to live there. That puny old closet of his wouldn't fit your summer wardrobe, much less his clothes and yours. You can't serve dinner to friends on TV trays. And there isn't a guest room.[15]

If these arguments prove unpersuasive, tell him that you simply could not cook dinner in his kitchen—which will set off some serious warning bells. Where would you put your cookbooks? And what about your food processor? Your stand mixer? Your juice extractor? Your pasta paddle? (The fancier the gadgets, the

---

[15]Whatever you do, don't mention your mother coming to visit, though.

more impressed he will be, so don't hold back.) If he offers to take you out to dinner every night, make sure to get a rain check, then remind him how expensive it would be, night after night. Besides, wouldn't he rather spend that money on power tools? When he wavers, start talking about your "special dishes"—you know, butternut squash soup, chicken cacciatore, blackberry scones. And don't worry if you've never cooked more than bologna in the microwave—just make sure to pronounce the names of these dishes with a modicum of credulity, and watch him drool. Later, when he's eating his tuna casserole, he won't remember.

As a last resort, you may have to pull out the big guns. If your husband grows adamant about staying in his place, tell him that without more closet space, you'll never have enough room for your lingerie. Which means that you'll—sigh!—have to throw away all of your skimpy bras, see-through panties and black lace teddies.

Trust me. He'll be on the phone to the real-estate agent in no time.

In My House

Ah, now this is better. You have the perfect home, so why shouldn't you and your new husband move right on in? Of course, you could always use a few more kitchen items, but since you never seem to use the ones you've got, that can wait until Christmas. Entertaining? You have a beautiful dining room. And you wouldn't say no to another set of china, but the patterns from your wedding registry are fine for now. Then again, a bigger table would be nice, what with all the holidays coming up. But you can always upsize during the next "no down payment, no interest" sale at your favorite furniture store.

Your bathroom has everything a woman could need, from the dressing table right down to the aromatherapy pillow in the bathtub. And your bedroom? Why, it's the coziest room in the house, with all forty-two pillows on your four-poster bed. Oh, the fun you'll have! What better than for two lovebirds to move into your perfect nest?

Well, I hate to break it to you, darlin', but even though moving into your place may seem like the ideal solution for newlyweds, it's much trickier than you think. First of all, your living room probably feels like a museum to him—a very scary museum where he will break and ruin the things you care most about. He won't want to, but he will. It's a leftover trait from childhood, and unfortunately, it will not be the first or the last time a husband destroys a precious object belonging to his wife. He won't think twice about setting his nice cold drink on top of your maple coffee table, without a coaster. He'll drag muddy boots across your carpet and set his dirty fanny on your silk sofa. He'll knock over your Tiffany lamp every time he walks by.

In fact, the more there is to break or destroy, the more a husband will cause you grief. Just ask my mother, who watched not one but two heirloom nineteenth-century cut-glass vases (which would have passed down to me and my sisters) shattered to smithereens by my stepfather, who until that moment did not understand why tossing a ball around the living room was a bad idea. All I can say is, sometimes it takes a little drama for men to get the point.

Another problem with your place is that men hate anything with a floral print. That doesn't mean your husband did not thoroughly enjoy making out with you on your Laura Ashley sofa while you were dating. He most certainly did, but he'll still look at you like you're insane if you so much as suggest that he watch a ball game from there with his buddies. Not that you would ever want to suggest such a thing, because doing so would mean regular gatherings at your place—not to mention the cost of re-covering that sofa in a few months, after the guys spill salsa and beer on it. However, the other option is equally disturbing, and I hope you look good in black. Because, if he can't ever watch games at your place, you're going to become a sports widow when he heads out to a less "embarassing" spot to watch them.

In addition to female florals, there is the problem of female pheromones. According to my husband, girls' houses "smell funny." When pressed to explain what he means by "funny," he said, "You know—perfumes, soaps, powders and candles." Oh, yes. And how nasty they do smell, right? Don't get me started on men and their smells—which I cover thoroughly in the chapter on hygiene. Suffice to say that there is a distinct difference between what men and women consider normal, when it comes to odors.

Other complaints that he is likely to have is that he can't find anything and he can't move anything at your place. After all, you don't keep duct tape in your silverware drawer now, do you? Not that he would find it, even if you did. Marital blindness is a common male affliction. Just wait.

And then there's your cat, which he could well despise. My sister's fiancé laid down the law—either he or the cat had to go—and I know he wasn't the first to do so, because I spotted a newspaper ad about this very situation. On the left of the ad was a picture of a cat. On the right was a picture of a man. Under the cat photo was the following description: *Adorable housetrained cat, 4 years old, very affectionate.* Under the husband's photo: *Handsome new husband, good handyman, friendly.* Then, under both, it said, in big, bold letters, *Husband insists either he or the cat must go—you choose which you want.*

Finally, let's not forget that even if your husband agrees to move into your place, he will have an entire apartment of stuff he'll want to bring with him. To me, that's scarier than Scott Peterson moving in next door. Seriously, where would you put all of his tools? And those weights? Oh, why can't he just go to the gym like everyone else?

Fortunately, it's highly unlikely your husband will want to move into your place, so you're probably safe. But if, by some strange chance, he does seem excited about the prospect, beware, beware, beware. It means that he (a) is out of a job; (b) is completely broke; (c) has just moved out of his mother's house; or (d) all of the above. In this case, you will become his mama, and may the Lord have mercy on you. All you can do is to try and turn him into a househusband (good luck) and get ready to support him for the next forty years.

Our House

Like the other two options, there are both advantages and disadvantages to finding a new place together. I am convinced, however, that the former far outweighs the latter. In fact, as far as I can see, the disadvantages of getting a new place together revolve primarily around two things: cleaning out and moving your stuff, and saying goodbye to old roommates.

Renting or buying a new place together is, first and foremost, an excellent opportunity to throw away unwanted junk. No matter how painful this can be (I personally prefer general anesthesia before submitting myself to the process), like most surgery—my mother's boob job not included—it is a necessary process. Besides, there is good money to be made in garage sales, not to mention the convenience of actually being able to see the back of your closet again.

A new place will also give you the perfect opportunity to

cement your status as a married couple. My mother-in-law described cleaning out her house as the process of defining herself. So, as you move into a new home with your new husband, you begin the process of defining yourself as a couple. I'm sure she would say that Mark and I have defined our couple as Hector the Collector meets Throw-It-Out Hal.

Something that is not so easily dispensed with is leaving the humble abode where you and your roommates have been happily cohabitating. It's not that they don't expect it, and it's certainly not that they aren't happy for you—they just aren't quite ready for it.

On the night you finally got engaged, your roommate was probably waiting up for you. You showed her your ring and you both burst into tears. You were crying with happiness. She was crying over a multitude of feelings: sadness over losing you, worry about how your future husband would treat you, and a tad bit of envy—which you certainly understand, having been there yourself.

Fortunately, her anxiety was quickly replaced by fear and dread over your plans for the bridesmaid dresses. Unlike her, during your excitement of picking a style that your bridesmaids would "definitely be able to wear again after the wedding" (probably to a Halloween party, no matter how much you think otherwise), you forgot all the underlying emotions she was going through. Then you moved out. She, on the other hand, was still very much aware of her feelings—every single one of them.

It's a little-known fact, but moving out on a roommate has been clinically proven to cause perfectly sane women to engage in psychotic behavior. Kind of like brides, actually. Under oath, however, we will all swear that it had absolutely nothing whatsoever to do with the pending wedding.

Several weeks before my big event, I moved into the new

apartment that Mark and I had chosen. It was only a few minutes' drive from the place I had shared with my adorable roommate—a Canadian gal with stunning, all-natural blond hair, perfect skin and a sense of humor to keep you howling. We had decorated our apartment on our meager student incomes, but it was cozy, and it was home. We held many a party there, too—my favorite being our annual War of 1812 shindig, where we divided the room into two halves, Canada and the United States, and decorated accordingly. Banana trees and fake flowers on my side; fake snow and stuffed birds on her side (hey, we had to make do with what we had—and her sister had married a taxidermist).

We'd bonded over countless late-night discussions. We'd shopped together, commiserated together, played pranks together. She was my closest friend, so it was with very mixed feelings that I told her I was getting married. After all, I was losing that special closeness we had shared for so long. But, unlike her, I was gaining a regular cuddle partner, my own personal accountant and someone to take care of me when I was sick.[16]

My roommate now had the unexpected burden of finding someone who was not only sane but who could also afford to pay her share of the rent. That's stressful in a way that choosing your wedding photographer definitely is not.

Two weeks before the wedding, in the midst of bridal showers and luncheons, I packed my things and moved out. A few days later, my roommate called and asked if I had mistakenly taken her red plastic kitchen spoon. When I figured out what spoon she was talking about, I agreed to look for it. Then, as I tend to, I forgot. For once in my life, I actually had a good excuse. Not only was I in the me-myself-and-I, prewedding, narcissistic frenzy that plagues all brides, but I also had yet to unpack my boxes. I'm bad about

[16]Well, two out of three, anyway.

unpacking. After trips, I typically pull out the dirty clothes and live from my suitcase for a few days.

My roommate called back the next day. I quickly picked through the boxes—to no avail. She hung up, frustrated, then called back a day or two later. This time, with the catering company on one line and the photographer on the other, I offered to replace it. After all, it was a plastic serving spoon worth no more than a buck or two. She refused. It was her favorite spoon, she said, and she needed it. She accused me of stealing it. I told her she was being obsessive. We argued. By the time the wedding rolled around, there was a distinct chill between us.

Fortunately, given other prewedding tensions that plagued us, Mark and I had a bevy of shrinks to call upon (something I highly recommend, in general, when it comes to marriage). We had gone through premarital counseling at our local church, which was a lot of fun—until we started fighting. We finished the course, did not get engaged as planned and followed advice to "get counseling from a professional." Sounds ominous, eh?

Fortunately, the ensuing sessions on the couch eventually led to an engagement and a wedding, but I would be remiss if I did not confess that two weeks after the honeymoon we started the first of what was to become a gabillion hours on the couch with that same professional. That's one of the reasons I'm writing this book—to hopefully save you that same investment of time and money, not to mention possibly going deaf from all the screaming, as my husband now seems to be. But, as it pertains to this story, I was fortunate, because advice about strange behavior was just a phone call away, or a mere $100 counseling appointment. I availed myself with regard to the spoon.

"She's grieving the loss of your friendship," our favorite shrink said. "And she doesn't realize it, but the spoon is her way of hanging on to you. It gives her an excuse to call you, and it provides a way to direct the anger she feels at being rejected, because she knows she can't show you that anger."

It made perfect sense. The spoon issue had gotten out of control, and neither of us knew what to do. So, a few weeks after the wedding, I drummed up the courage to call her. We went out to lunch, and I asked if maybe, just maybe—and this was just a thought, something I was wondering about—she was perhaps feeling sad about my leaving and possibly channeling those feelings into the . . . uh . . . the spoon?

She thought about it, then burst into tears. That must be it, she said. She was sorry. No, I was sorry. We both apologized a dozen times for being insensitive, then made up. Now, even though we live on opposite sides of North America, I still consider her one of my best friends.

But, as luck would have it, she was right all along. To my abject horror, I found that stupid spoon three years after the wedding, when we had finally unpacked all of those boxes and moved to the opposite coast. So, Anita, I'm a big fat idiot—and I owe you a set of kitchen utensils.

Fortunately, men do not have abandonment issues that manifest themselves through objects. They also do not have roommate issues that are tantamount to marriage problems. After your husband popped the all-important question to you, he announced to his mother, his best friend and his dog that he was engaged, then went back to business as usual. If he's like most men, he probably neglected to tell his roommate, who was out of town at the time. But as soon as he knew the wedding was definitely going through— that is, the morning of your wedding day—he finally remembered to tell his roommate. The roommate, who happened to be putting on his tux at the time, thanked him for the reminder, slapped him on the back and called a few friends. Then, before you walked down the aisle, your husband's roommate already had someone lined up and ready to move in.

The same je ne sais quoi attitude (that's French for "We have spoons?") prevails with regard to shared objects. If your husband were to mistakenly pack one of his roommate's kitchen utensils, neither he nor the roommate would probably ever notice. Not only that, but neither of them would recognize it when you pulled it out of the box and wondered aloud where it came from. This would prove true even if the utensil in question was an heirloom sterling silver spoon with a mother-of-pearl handle that had been passed down through generations of the roommate's family since the Revolutionary War, and which was mistakenly left in the bottom of the roommate's laundry box, which he took home.

This, by the way, would be one of the rare times that you would actually want to keep something that arrives in a box from your husband's previous address.

THREE

The Decorating War:
Black and White

O h, how I wish I could tell you how much fun it will be to decorate your little love nest together. Truly I do. But the sad fact of the matter is, unless your decorating tastes lean toward superheros or beers of the world—or unless your husband is gay, in which case you need far more help than this book—there's about as much chance as a blizzard in Biloxi that you and your beloved will agree on these things. After all, what does a woman who enjoys color, style and harmony have in common with someone who keeps dumbbells in the dining room?

It doesn't matter if your new husband is as country as cornflakes or a tenth-generation Yankee. Men just do not see decor the way we do. If you're already married, you've been through the China Wars (as well as the Crystal Wars and Silver Wars) which, naturally, you won hands down, before the wedding. After all, like many Southern Girls, you probably picked out your patterns in the third grade, with no small amount of prodding from your grandmother—who just happens to have the same pattern and who has promised to leave it to you. Talk about incentive.

But, precisely because your husband surrendered on those battle fronts, in order to get down that aisle and enjoy your nuptial fruits, he's not about to give in again. Not for any of the big decorating decisions, anyway. After all, there's his male pride to consider, which makes the great state of Texas look tiny. He also has some serious turf to regain. Now, in a few years, he won't give a fig about this sort of thing. He'll happily sit on a chintz couch in a pink living room with scented jasmine candles and not even notice when a dried flower arrangement falls on his head. But right now, it's an out-and-out battle for territory.

If you don't believe me, just ask the people at HGTV. Their hit reality show, *Decorating for the Sexes*, is based on this very premise. Producers hit upon a gold mine when they realized that couples would go to war over whether to keep the cork coffee table the husband had found in his Dumpster. Take it from a woman who had to live with what came to be known as "the West Virginia sofa"—a high-backed, scratchy love seat covered in brown fabric with orange and yellow flowers, which bore a striking resemblance to the one Ellie Mae and Granny rode atop their truck in *The Beverly Hillbillies*. My new husband thought that love seat was just fine. I hid every time a repairman arrived.

It's all a matter of perspective. When you say, "What a gorgeous sage green sofa," your new husband will say, "Looks like vomit to me." When you point out the smooth-and-easy comfort of a chenille accent chair, he'll talk about durability, and steer you to the leather section (if not the pleather, bless his taste-deprived heart). You perceive "depth" in modern art. He insists a toddler could do better. It's a never-ending process that could drive you to do what one Southern Girl did. She told her stubborn new husband that he could keep his nasty old mattress. Then she fixed it for him, all nice and cozy. In the garage.

But take heart. As with many newlywed issues, this, too, will end—just as soon as he sees your point of view. In other words, once he gets tired of going to furniture stores and spending long hours with decorators and salesmen. But that takes time. In the meantime, he's still trying to mark his territory, while you need something to sit on. And a smelly, stained recliner is not what you had in mind.

Long before you purchase or arrange anything, however, you must purge.

Goodbye

Getting rid of your husband's things is a very important process that must be undertaken with the same attention that you need to repair a run in your panty hose at a black-tie event. It must be done carefully, swiftly and behind closed doors. Now, depending on your husband's taste, or lack thereof, you will probably want to keep some items. His clothes, for example. (Well, most of them, anyway—we'll deal with wardrobe issues in a later chapter.) His four-burner, deluxe stainless-steel grill might also come in handy. And, since he's probably still paying for it, you should probably take the $10,000 surround-sound stereo. Don't forget the fire extinguisher—an important safety item. However, you'll need to explain that, just because the canister "matches" the dining room doesn't mean it goes there.

Husband's Belongings to Keep

- Select items of clothing
- Four-burner, deluxe stainless-steel grill
- $10,000 surround-sound stereo
- Fire extinguisher

Other items can be more tricky. To figure out which ones should remain, you'll need to get rid of your husband for a day or two prior to the move, while gaining access to his things. After all, you can't sift through his stuff with him looking over your shoulder. But first, you'll need to spend time observing his behavior in his natural habitat. Notice which coffee mug he reaches for again and again—and which ones remain at the back of the cabinet. Pay particular attention to the clothes he likes to wear. Look for recurring patterns.

Make sure to avoid things that have both emotional and financial significance. For example, he would probably consider his faded, ripped BOSTON T-shirt a "sentimental" item, because the band broke up and never played after their second album. It's of zero financial value, however—and extremely embarrassing—so it will go. The pristine NASCAR program signed by the late Dale Earnhardt, on the other hand, is definitely a keeper.

Things that are safe to get rid of are the worst of his clothing: ancient underwear, socks with holes, shoes you haven't seen him wear during the last year and embarrassing hats—unless they pertain to sports, of course (which means baseball caps of any kind). You can also safely toss hotel towels, hotel sheets, hotel ashtrays, hotel soaps and hotel shampoos. If he has hotel furniture, however, you may have a problem.

As a general rule, all sports equipment is off-limits, as is any-thing electronic made after the year 2000 (just in case). I personally take issue with items that contain antlers, teeth or fur—although these things could come in handy when decorating your mountain cabin someday. You might also want to consider keeping any furni-ture that could fetch a fair price, no matter how ugly. Remember, there are a lot of single men out there who shop at garage sales, looking for ugly furniture (think "West Virginia Sofa").

Also off-limits are his collections, no matter how pointless they may seem. Now by "collections," I do not necessarily mean more than one item. My husband, for example, has a special baseball that he considers part of a collection. That he only has one baseball is ir-relevant, as is the fact that he has never added to "his collection." He intends to collect more. Fine. I can live with one baseball. It stays in his study, atop a coin jar. On the other hand, your husband may have a collection of five hundred action figures, each with its own special box, as one Southern Girl's husband does. Houseguests sleep on the sofa. His action figures? They get their own bedroom.

So beware the collections of men. And don't have a hissy fit when he starts talking about building display shelves for his two-hundred-plus bottles of hot sauce. There will be a time and a place to get rid of these, down the road.

Important Dates to Remember for Purging

- **October to June:** Basketball Season
- **April to October:** Baseball Season
- **September to January:** Football Season
- **October to June:** Hockey Season

Having completed your first run-through of items, you will need to figure out which sport your husband obsesses about most. Fortunately, this will not be difficult. Even if his favorite sport is out of season, you can probably persuade him to watch another one.[17] If he enjoys multiple sports (and what man doesn't), you're home free. Just make sure you keep a straight face when you suggest he hit his favorite sports bar for the big game. Tell him that you're going to spend the day cleaning, and that he should stay gone for a while—unless he wants to help.

On the big day, arm yourself with a set of stickers. (A few bottles of air freshener probably wouldn't hurt, either.) I suggest color coding according to urgency. For example, use red stickers for those items that must be disposed of before the move, orange stickers for things you intend to lose and/or break during the move and green stickers for those that you plan to keep temporarily.

Color Code for Disposal of Husband's Possessions

- **Red Stickers:** Items to dispose of before the move
- **Orange Stickers:** Items to lose and/or break during the move
- **Green Stickers:** Items to keep temporarily

Here's how to handle the red items. Place the smaller items in boxes and, together with the "furniture" (cinder blocks, boards, 1960s pleather recliner), put everything in a corner of the basement

---

[17]Yeah—how hard will that be?

or garage. Next make a list of those items, carefully noting the most objectionable characteristics of each one (rust stains on the tattered Motel 6 towel, for example). Finally, purchase two tickets to the finals of his favorite game. Put the tickets into an envelope and make a nice (large) dinner.

When he comes home, serve him dinner and tell him that you're going to play *Let's Make a Deal*. Hand him the game tickets, have him open the envelope and tell him that these are Door Number One. Enjoy the look on his face. Next lead him to Door Number Two, with his pile of stuff. Show him the list of objectionable characteristics. Point to them. When he looks confused, explain that he has a choice. He can either keep the curry-scented orange love seat and its matching friends, or he can go to the March Madness finals. Trust me. His buddies will be hauling his junk to the dump in less time than it takes to say, "Chili cheese dog, fries and a beer, please."

Getting rid of the orange-stickered items is the next step, and it must be undertaken with great care and consideration. First, pack the breakables in boxes without bubble wrap, using as little newspaper as possible—just enough to make it look as if they are ready to be transported. Other targets will include dishes and glassware, his beer-bottle collection and perhaps some of those excess photos of Mama. As for photos of ex-girlfriends, we have a very special way to deal with those (see below).

On moving day, take these boxes—along with any other items you want destroyed, like his mother's table lamp—and place them in the car, truck or moving van that your husband will be driving. They will need to be placed toward the back. If your husband has the foresight and the skills to pack everything in tightly—unlikely, but it has been known to happen—you will need to go behind him and undo his handiwork. Then watch him take off. He probably won't make it past the first speed bump before it's all happily destroyed.[18] If he complains, remind him who was driving.

For orange-stickered furniture, slip the movers a little something while your husband is in the bathroom. Then use subtle signs—like vigorous head shaking and frantic throat-slitting motions—to cue them what should "go" and what should be moved. Believe me, they'll be more than happy to cart off your leftovers, after the big move. And when your husband looks perplexed at his missing cinder-block "entertainment center," just shrug your shoulders. It's amazing what gets lost in the move these days.

Once all the boxes have arrived, you will need to sort through them and decide what to keep. Your husband will, no doubt, want to be involved, which will turn a five-hour process into an eighty-five-hour process. Here's what to do. As you open each box and remove an item, make sure to find the same item in another box before making a decision. Tell him that this is the only way you can do it, by comparing and contrasting. How else will you know which frying pan to keep? Yours or his? Remember, you don't want too many pots now.

He'll squirm, but as soon as he sees the two pans, side by side, he'll be forced to admit that your clean one is much nicer than his dirty one. Poof! Into the box marked GARAGE SALE goes his frying pan. Next pull out his spaghetti pot and go searching for yours. Then compare once again. What does he think? Before long, he'll get bored and wander out of the kitchen. At that point, you can just take the rest of his things—after searching for any unlikely treasures, of course—and dump them all into the garage-sale box.

---

[18]Of course, convincing him to throw out the broken items once you arrive in your new home is another matter entirely.

In addition to forcing you to deal with old things, moving in together is also a time for new things—and that means doing what you, dear Southern Girl, do best: shopping! Unfortunately, however, your husband will probably want to join you—and that can put a damper on things. After all, it's not like shopping with a man is fun (even if he's paying). Unlike women, men view shopping as a hunt, you see—not an experience. Their goal is to find, track and kill a new dining room table as quickly as possible. In other words, still new to the joys of marriage, your husband will assume that shopping for new furniture and decorative household items is fun, just like a hunt. It is your job to relieve him of this misconception.

Fortunately, that is not a difficult task. It simply means doing what women were born to do, and that is shop. And shop. And shop. Just be sure to bring the antianxiety medication for him, while you do, though.

Every Little Thing

Southern Girls are raised around the concept of "home," and home is sovereign ground—so let anyone who comes near it, therefore, beware. Sadly, it can take a new husband several years before he figures out just how treacherous these waters are, however. It is up to you to show him this as soon as possible.

The first thing a new husband must realize is that a man's home is not his castle. We don't know who said this, but they were wrong, wrong, wrong. A man might own the castle, pay the mortgage on the castle and even be required to clean the castle, but he is never allowed to decorate the castle. Now you can appease his frustration about this by explaining that houses have male and female rooms. A man's sovereign domain includes the garage, the attic, the basement, the yard (minus any flowers), the shed, the deck (in particular, the grill, which will allow him to get in touch with his inner caveman) and the exterior of the house. In other words, your husband is allowed to decorate any room or area that does not have central heat or air-conditioning.

Areas where he has absolutely no say include the kitchen, the dining room, the living room, the guest bedroom and bathroom, the front porch, the laundry room, hall closets and various nooks and crannies. He will want some say in the TV room, his office and the master bedroom, but only to a certain degree. If he insists on all masculine colors, just take him to the stores and start pondering the options. In addition to dishes, towels, bath mats, bedspreads and furniture, don't forget to look at wallpaper samples and window treatments during your shopping expedition. Take your time. And as soon as he sees something he likes, just pull out a few more selections. He'll be begging for mercy in no time.

The Bertha Butt Boogie

These days, it's highly unlikely that you are the first girl your husband has ever loved. And with those previous relationships comes baggage. Not only emotional baggage, but physical baggage. Photos, letters, rings, watches, sweaters, stuffed animals—you name it. They all serve to remind him of the past. And if you let them, those little reminders will drive you nuts. Getting rid of them is, therefore, a key factor in keeping your sanity after marriage. It won't be easy, but with the grace and aplomb of a Southern Girl, you can make a clean sweep of anything that might remind him of Those Who Have Come Before.

Photos

For women, this is a no-brainer. We do not want our husband looking at Miss Thang for the rest of eternity. She's the past, we're the present and that's all there is to it. But sometimes, when setting up house for the first time, old photos have a way of appearing. It is up to you to make those photos disappear.

The reason is simple. No matter how much of a beauty queen we may be now, time has a way of taking its toll. My mother used to say that after the age of forty, a woman has to choose between her face and her figure. I scoffed. Then I started the downhill slide toward forty. Of course, they have perfected the art of liposuction and face-lifts during the last few years, which I shall have no moral qualms about embracing someday (despite my protests to the contrary, when I was a wee child of twenty-five). After all, even the best of us will eventually get crow's-feet and, God forbid, stretch marks.

Now the fact that your husband's ex probably has an eighties hairdo and three kids clinging to her thunder thighs is likely to elude him. No doubt, she remains forever frozen in time, wearing her itsy-bitsy, teeny-weeny bikini and grinning like a drunken hyena on the beach in Fort Lauderdale. And I think we have enough problems in life without having to face that, too, now, don't we? Remember, men's memories are selective enough without any photos to mislead them. Because I promise you, dear Southern Girl, that during those seasons when you are not so itsy-bitsy—like the third trimester of your third pregnancy—you just might not want him leering, especially at someone who doesn't even exist anymore.

Second, in addition to reminding him of the ex and their relationship, photos of her tend to serve as reminders of the glory days. Now you and I both know that those days were not really glorious. They may tell themselves that chasing women, wearing togas and imitating an alligator on the beer-slopped floor of a fraternity house made for good times, but we know that is an illusion. For the most part, these boys were like the prodigal son who threw away his inheritance and ended up eating pig slop. Eventually, the hangovers became worse than the high, the bar tabs more than the tuition and the relationships more than they could handle. When they married us, they came home, and we're throwing them the best party they ever had. They know this. And they appreciate it. But removing any reminders from the old days won't hurt.

One exception to this rule must be mentioned, however, and that is husbands who have children from a first marriage. Whether through death or divorce, their whole world has been shattered, and displaying a photo or two of the children's mother should be a given. With most Southern Girls, this will not be an issue. We are full of mercy and compassion, and we would never allow selfishness or jealousy to stand in the way of a child's love for his mother— even if she is a dragon. Besides, you can always insist that the photos remain in the children's bedroom. And you can keep that door closed when they are not around.

For the rest of us, drastic measures must be taken. Fortunately, men don't usually wax nostalgic about the past the way we do. In fact, the longer they're married, the less likely they are to remember the past at all.[19] Men also tend to be a bit more in touch with their anger than us, so the photos are often the first to go—usually in a fit of rage. This can be very cathartic, and if you are one of the lucky girls whose husband has succumbed to the search-and-destroy theory of ex-girlfriends, count yourself among the blessed.

[19]Meaning, anything that happened in the last five minutes.

If you are not, however, never fear. You can be the one to introduce him to the shredder.

Early on in my relationship with Mark, he took me home to meet his mother. During our visit, he discovered an old box of photos of his ex in the garage. Apparently, Mark had already destroyed most of them (I was impressed), but some loose ones had somehow survived.

In a gesture that sealed our fate and left me with no doubt as to his unswerving loyalty, Mark grabbed the box and tossed it into the trash. (I now realize, in hindsight, that this was an early warning sign of his obsession with throwing things out.) Curious girl that I am, I stopped him. I wanted to see those photos, even if I hated everything about them. So we looked, and he told me—the vacation in Bermuda, their trip to England, her dog, her sister, her sister's dog—you get the idea. It was everything I could do not to hurl myself out the window. Fortunately, however, he spoke without one iota of regret. Then I had an idea, and I promise you that I had no ill motives whatsoever.

"Mark," I said, "what if, instead of just throwing these photos away, you tore the two of you apart? As a symbol?"

He liked the idea. "You mean like this?" he said, ripping a close-up in half and grinning.

With that, he began tearing up those photos as fast as he could, carefully pulling the two of them apart before shredding the rest. He even invited me to join him, which turned it into a healing experience. Mark regained some of the power he had lost during their breakup, then closed the door on his past. I leaned against that door and sighed with relief. We were engaged three months later.

Symbols are powerful. It's the reason we cry when they play the national anthem. It's the reason we have our children baptized, even if we don't attend church. It's the reason the flag was flaunted by so many people after 9/11. And it's the reason we take pictures: to remind us of what is most important. So if your husband has photos of old girlfriends, break out a bottle of wine and suggest a shredding session. It just might turn into a party, complete with confetti. And if he doesn't go for the idea, remember, accidents have been known to happen.

Other Possessions

In addition to photos, your husband is likely to have a little collection of items from previous relationships with women. This is my rule: If he can remember who it came from within a few seconds, it should definitely go. Unless it has great value, that is, in which case you should auction it on eBay. The most important thing is to assess just how attached your husband is to the various items he has managed to acquire. You then must determine how much you can live with—and whether the object in question is worth it.

My husband managed to extract the everyday dishes, silverware and a set of crystal wineglasses from his ex. Amazingly, he also got to keep the china, which was outrageously expensive (more outrageously expensive than most china, even), although he later gave it to the wonderful woman who mothered him and gave him a place to live after the breakup. Which was just fine with me, since there were only six place settings.[20]

We are still using his everyday dishes and silverware, although I can't say I am disappointed when one of those fortunately discontinued dishes happens to break. I have a problem with the wineglasses, however. I am not quite sure why. They're a lovely

---

[20]Kidding! She totally deserved that china. (Anybody who would house and feed my husband does.)

Lenox pattern that looks just like Waterford, and I love Waterford. But I positively hate those glasses. Mark, however, refuses to drink wine out of anything else. Recently, he's even started drinking water from them. So far, I've stifled my urge to make them disappear, but I must also confess that we have an ever-growing selection of new wineglasses to choose from, and choose I do. It's a woman's prerogative, after all.

In addition to these household items, Mark also had a gold designer watch when I first met him—a gift from his ex. It was Cartier, and he loved it. I, on the other hand, despised it. But I happened to have had a very nice Rolex from one of my ex-boyfriends, so I didn't push the issue. As Kenny Rogers once said, ya gotta know when to hold 'em.

FOUR

Husbands and Hygiene: The Night the Lights Went Out in Georgia

W hen it comes to comparisons between men and women, nowhere is the gap more vast than in the matter of hygiene. "Oh, why can't a woman be like a man?" asked Henry Higgins in *My Fair Lady*. The answer, of course, is that if she were, the entire planet Earth—and perhaps a few others in the galaxy as well—would collapse, in a matter of months, under the mountains of mold and mildew that the solitary male population would create.

Cleanliness—or the lack thereof—is a uniquely personal subject, and under ordinary circumstances, I would be loath to raise such an issue, much less engage in a lengthy discussion about it. It is simply not what a Southern Girl does. We learn, of course, because we must, about things like flushing the toilet and running the faucet (to camouflage sounds), at a very young age, during the potty-training years. Henceforth, however, those things cease to exist. We do them, but we do them in private, and we don't talk about them.

When it pertains to soon-to-be-weds and newlyweds, however, I find myself compelled to broach the subject. Otherwise, you may find yourselves in an abject state of shock.

Bathrooms exist for two reasons: to clean oneself and to relieve oneself. Fortunately, men do both, which means that husbands will do both—at least most of the time. One Southern Girl tearfully confessed to me, months after her wedding, that her new husband did not believe in taking showers—at least on a daily basis. Now we're not sure what neck of the woods he was raised in (perhaps the woods, indeed), but that sort of thing is not Southern at all. Southern Boys certainly like to sweat, but they scrub up beautifully—even if they do leave the shower in a state of chaos. Her husband, however, was clearly an exception to this rule—and he's lucky we're not naming names. Jerry.

His wife, a dear Southern Girl if ever there was one, confronted him—rather loudly, I might add—about this habit. He did not see the problem. She begged, she pleaded, she cajoled—to no avail. Finally, after he refused to shower before the wedding rehearsal of a family member, she went ballistic. Alas, it is not uncommon for Southern Girls to lose their tempers and throw hissy fits.

I learned about the problem only because I happened to knock on the door of their hotel room at the same moment that she came storming out. I suggested that she buy an expensive bottle of cologne (I happen to be partial to Polo) and spray him with it whenever they went out. To my amazement, it actually worked. She starting spraying, he started showering and we all breathed a sigh of relief. Of course, she also told him that on days when he did not shower, conjugal rights would not be exercised, which may have been a tad more persuasive than the cologne.

Which leads us to the first—and least distasteful—reason for the existence of bathrooms: keeping oneself clean. Now there are theories upon theories about cleanliness, but I am convinced that North Americans have the highest standards in the world for this sort of thing. So if you've married a Frenchman, dear Southern Girl, I do hope he does not come from the proletariat masses who use less than one bar of soap a year (trust me, the others do shower and shave like the rest of us). If he's British, I hope that he's had his teeth fixed, as that tends to be a rather glaring problem in that part of the world. As for other countries, you are on your own.

For most Southern Girls, however, it is not the issue of whether their husbands clean and/or relieve themselves, but how they do it.

I Can't Help Myself

After carefully using the toilet, which many of us still call the commode, a Southern Girl will do a brief inspection of the bowl. If any, shall we say, "debris" is left behind, she will take care of it with the help of the nearby designer toilet brush. The thought of someone using the commode after her, without it being perfectly clean, would be more horrifying than a Kentucky Derby party without hats. And, of course, a Southern Girl always flushes. I'll never forget being in a public bathroom one time and hearing a Southern Girl exclaim, from the stall beside me, "What is it with people not flushing the dang toilet? I learned that when I was two years old!"

Indeed.

After flushing, a Southern Girl will spray the room with air freshener. She'll sniff and spray again, for good measure. Finally, she will wash her hands with a fruit-scented designer soap, finishing with a squirt of correlating hand lotion, located next to the sink.

Bathroom Goals

For a woman: Go as quietly as possible and leave the bathroom as clean as possible, finishing (hopefully) in less than thirty minutes.
For a man: Go as quickly as possible and have a little fun, while practicing his "aim."

A man, on the other hand, views going to the bathroom as a little game. The commode is the target; his pee[21] is the dart. When he aims, he points in the general direction of that target and hopes for the best. Sometimes he hits, sometimes he misses. If he happens to be yawning during his "throw," well, there's always next time.

After most men use the bathroom, it would not occur to them to partake of one of the hygienic aloe wipes that have been thoughtfully provided by his wife and placed next to the commode, in plain view. And, if a man happens to notice any of the yellow stains he has just created—unlikely, but it has been known to happen—he will probably assume they're part of the decor. As for any debris, well, that would be the maid's job. You did know you were a maid, didn't you? Your credentials arrived in the mail, honey, along with your name-change documents.

Flushing, of course, is something that men were taught by

[21]When referring to human urine, Southern Girls may use either "tee-tee" or "pee," depending on the circumstances. "Tee-tee" is a more delicate terminology, and tends to be used in polite company or with small children, for purposes of potty training. "Pee," on the other hand, is slightly more derogatory. Thus, if a Southern Girl wishes to show disdain for something—for example, the act of urinating on a seat, without cleaning it up—she will use the word "pee."

their mamas, so they take care to do that. Except, of course, when they forget. And hand washing? That's for amateurs.

Shower the People

When it comes to showering, a typical Southern Girl will use several hair products formulated from a variety of edible items that include kiwis, bergamot and extract of coriander; rare essential oils like rose petal, frankincense and ylang-ylang; and a host of vitamins that may or may not exist. For this privilege, she will pay her hairdresser a monthly wage that would feed the population of several developing countries for an entire year. Her shampoo, which will have a matching designer conditioner, will have been specially blended for Southern sun damage.

She will use reconstructive-hair-surgery hot oil once a week, for reversal of blow-drying effects, and will require at least twenty minutes of conditioning time. Her facial puff will be woven from completely natural fibers taken from the Nile River, and her facial cleanser—made to be used in conjunction with the all-natural Nile facial puff—will be made of Egyptian seaweed strands specially blended for her level of oily skin. The correlating revitalizing mask, made of crushed seashells from the Indian Ocean, will follow.

While waiting for the face mask to extract the impurities from her skin, she will shave her underarms, feet, toes, ankles, calves, knees and upper thighs, using a feminine shaving cream and a six-blade angled razor made just for women, to fit all of their curves. After rinsing her hair of conditioner and rubbing off the face mask, she will scrub the rest of her body using a special exfoliating glove dipped in a rare body scrub used only by an ancient Far East sect—until recently discovered by her hairdresser, during his trip to Tibet. She will finish her shower using a baby-soft body cloth filled with oatmeal and almond body cleanser. Finally, she will attack the dead, dry skin from her feet and heels with a pumice stone, making sure that everything disappears into the drain.

After a thorough examination of her body for signs of unwelcome visitors, she will slather herself with body lotion, rub her feet with extra-emollient massage ointment, check her toenails and make a mental note to call the nail salon for a pedicure. She will then use an age-defying cream made of collagen for her face, tweeze her eyebrows and blow-dry, flatten and curl her hair. She will spend the next thirty minutes applying makeup and getting dressed, after which she will carefully hang up her towel to dry.

Two hours and fifteen minutes will have passed.

Her husband will have a very different routine. In the shower stall, it will not occur to him to look for a washcloth. He will freely pour his wife's extract-of-citrus Provençal body soap onto his hand, dribbling most into the drain. After knocking several beauty products onto the floor, which he will ignore, he will grab the first shampoo he can find, which will inevitably be the most expensive brand his wife has ever purchased—the one that was mixed by a rare tribe of virgins in the Yucatán Peninsula and recommended by her hairdresser to cure split ends. He will apply half the bottle to his hair. Fortunately, however, he will not use any conditioner.

Before turning off the shower, he will check to make sure his wife is not in the bathroom, then pee,[22] vaguely wondering where the shower pipe meets up with the toilet pipe under the house. After traipsing water throughout the bathroom, he will grab the first thing he sees—the embroidered linen hand towels his wife purchased during their honeymoon to Switzerland—and dry himself off.

---

[22]Please disregard all previous statements with regard to the appropriate use of the word "tee-tee." Women have a tee-tee and they tee-tee with their tee-tees. Boys tee-tee, too. Men and dogs, on the other hand, pee.

Later, he will complain that they are too small and not absorbent. He will then throw the wet towels onto the bed before spending two minutes getting dressed.

Exactly ten minutes will have passed. But at least he will be clean.

To save your marriage from beauty-product-induced bankruptcy, drastic measures must be taken. If, like my husband, yours can be persuaded that Suave is a designer label, you're home free. On the other hand, if he's somewhat savvy about hair care—say he

---

Cost of One Shower:

For a Woman:

Designer shampoo and conditioner	$2.25
Reconstructive hot oil hair surgery	$3.75
Facial Cleanser	$2.25
Revitalizing Mask	$2.50
Feminine Shaving Cream	$0.50
Body Scrub	$1.25
Body Cleanser	$1.25
Body Lotion	$1.75
Foot Ointment	$1.00
Age-Defying Face Cream	$8.75
Total Cost:	$25.25[23]

---

[23]Does not include onetime costs of all-natural facial puff ($21), six-blade angled women's razor ($9), exfoliating glove ($6), body cloth ($9), pumice stone ($4), manicure and pedicure equipment ($35), blow-dryer ($75), hair iron ($75), curlers ($30) and curling iron ($35).

For a Man:

Ivory Soap:	$ 0.08
Half bottle of designer shampoo (used by mistake instead of store brand)	$ 14.00
Reconstructive hot oil hair surgery (knocked over in shower)	$ 25.00
Age-defying face cream (stepped on outside shower)	$120.00
Total Cost:	$159.08

spent a bit too much time with Mama at the beauty parlor growing up—you'll need some imagination. Wait until your designer shampoo and conditioner bottles are empty (don't worry—it won't be long). Then fill them with your local grocery-store brand. Of course, this means that you'll need to keep the real designer bottles hidden, taking them out whenever you need them. But that's what you get for marrying a metrosexual.

As for his little "number ones" in the shower, you might try telling him that you've scoured the tiles with a special urine-detecting cleanser. As soon as any urine hits the shower stall, it will turn a hideous and permanent shade of purple, which you will require him to clean. This will only work once, however. As you may have already discovered, men love to test the limits.

Do Ya Think I'm Sexy?

Showers are not the only area where men and women differ, when it comes to personal hygiene. Some men appear to treat teeth brushing as an annoyance, for example. And mouthwash, I am convinced, was probably used on more than one occasion during their bachelor days as a way of getting out of that little requirement. So besmitten were you with his adorable little dimples that you simply failed to notice. Now that you are married, however, you will need to be on the lookout for husbands who perceive this three-minute activity as something that cuts into their free time.

It may therefore behoove you to explain the consequences of such foods as garlic (eaten solo, of course) and raw onions (oh, joy) on your husband's breath. And, believe it or not, you may also have to explain that just because he's not disturbed by your bad breath does not mean that you will not be bothered by his. It's a complicated concept, to be sure. Second, and depending upon the food consumed, you may also need to explain the very sophisticated technique of "gargle, then brush" to dear Hubby.

One husband came up with a singularly memorable excuse for his laziness in this area. When asked why he had not brushed his teeth—yet again—he replied, "I'm giving them a rest." Another husband had the opposite problem. Although fastidious when it came to oral hygiene, he nevertheless could not fathom why his wife hated kissing him after he had brushed his teeth and gargled—with Listerine. So, unless you enjoy medicinal kisses, it might be a good idea to put a nice bottle of amaretto-flavored mouthwash in his Christmas stocking.

If all else fails, I suggest you resort to the tried-and-true method of persuasion: slinking into the bedroom wearing your sexiest lingerie. When he perks up, run down the list. "Teeth brushed, mmmh? Mouthwash?" He will, no doubt, scurry into that bathroom as fast as you have ever seen him move. And don't complain if he takes a few extra minutes—he's no doubt taking care of some other hygienic issue that you have yet to notice.

The rest of the time—mornings before work, for example, when lovemaking isn't always practical—poses its own unique set of problems. Many husbands of Southern Girls rightly perceive the importance of brushing their teeth, yet still behave like pigs in their pens while doing so. My husband has a truly original way of brushing his. For Mark, bending over to spit out his toothpaste any less than five feet from the sink would be tantamount to launching a rocket from his lap. The greater the distance, the better the throw.

For many new brides, there is also the problem of conjugal audio activity in the bathroom. By this, I mean the male sounds that awaken us in the early hours of the morning, keep us awake at night and make us wonder why we ever thought men were sexy. My husband doesn't wait to get to the bathroom to begin his noises. Upon waking at five forty-five a.m. each morning (after hitting the snooze alarm no less than three times, I might add), he proceeds to shout at the top of his lungs—once, twice. The first weeks of marriage, I heard this and awoke screaming, certain that a murderer had entered our bedroom. Alas, my dear husband was merely clearing his nostrils. He calls it "sneezing," and he has done it twice in a row, every morning, for the past twelve years. He occasionally sneezes throughout the day as well, causing passersby to wonder if they should dial 911.

Other husbands like to gargle, clear their sinuses or blow their noses with great velocity. One Southern Girl compared her husband's sinus activity to a barking dog. Another described it as a loud gunshot. Still another insisted that her husband's nose blowing sounded like a gaggle of geese landing in the bathroom each morning. And one Southern Girl's husband left so many globs of toothpaste attached to the sink that she threatened to chip them off and serve them as after-dinner mints. Oh, and what about hairs and other unmentionables? I'm sorry. I can't even go there.

She Blinded Me with Science

Toilet seats, I am convinced, were invented by God to teach women patience and creativity. Patience, because toilet seats will haunt us wherever we go, regardless of how well we train our husbands. And creativity, because we must learn to "think outside the commode" when it comes to persuading men to put the stupid thing down.

Growing up, I did not encounter this problem. Both my father and stepfather had been well- and duly-trained by my mother, and I rarely saw the underside of a toilet seat. Therefore, it is hard to convey the shock that awaited me on my honeymoon and thereafter—especially when I realized that men are actually starting to fight back. Certain men in my family have even challenged me about why *they* should be the ones to put down the toilet seat, rather than women putting it up. Good gracious. To say that the gallant-knight era is dead would be an understatement. However, each time a man questions the necessity of this minor but greatly appreciated act, I simply sigh, then set about educating the man on the basics of potty training. Has he ever fallen into the toilet bowl in the middle of the night, I ask, because a woman has not put up the seat for him? Of course not. End of discussion.

I am fortunate when it comes to toilet seats, because Mark is very respectful. He puts them down most of the time, and now, after years of my tutelage (that's French for "deprivation of food and water"), he has acquired a near-perfect record. This is in direct contrast to my father-in-law, who annihilates years of hard work whenever he visits with constant visual reminders that leaving the seat up is actually an option. As we all know, it is not. But like so many other things on the steep learning curve of matrimony, this is something men must eventually accept.

For the most part, I will assume that, even with proper parental potty training, multiple years of bachelorhood will have left your husband at least somewhat delinquent in this area. Therefore, continuing adult education is needed. First, however, you must analyze the way that your husband processes information.

There are three primary learning styles to consider. Visual learners learn through seeing or reading. Audio learners learn through hearing. And tactile, or "kinesthetic," learners learn through doing, moving or touching.

Learning Styles of Husbands

- **Visual Learners:** Those who learn through seeing or reading
- **Auditory Learners:** Those who learn through hearing
- **Tactile/Kinesthetic Learners:** Those who learn through doing, moving and/or touching
- **Divorced Learners:** Those who never learned

To teach your visual-minded husband the fine art of the toilet-seat put-down, write him a casual reminder note. I'm partial to **PUT THE SEAT DOWN, HONEY!!!** in bold red ink. Wearing plastic gloves (it's treacherous under there), adhere the note to the underside of the toilet seat with oversized transparent tape. Make sure that it is front and center, at the top of the seat, so it's in full view when your husband raises the seat.

This strategy worked extremely well for me one year when we were housing an international student who came from a country where, clearly, women didn't dare ask men for this little courtesy. No matter how much I pleaded, this young man refused to "remember." To my immense relief, however, as soon as I put up the note, the toilet seat started going down. I'm not sure if I ever got through to the student, though. Mark later admitted that he was so worried about offending the young man that he spent a significant amount of time troubleshooting with the seat.

Now that's training for ya, ladies!

If you loathe the thought of touching the underside of the toilet seat, even with gloves (and who could blame you?), you can tape the note on the toilet tank, in plain view. Although you'll suffer some embarrassment when guests use your restroom, at least the male ones will put down the seat. You will also, by the way, be setting a stellar example in toilet-seat training for your female guests, especially the younger ones. Remember, gals: pay it forward.

The second part of your strategy for the visual learner involves a reminder, for those times when the note does not suffice. Purchase and install a strobe light over the bathroom door—the brighter, the better. You will need to rig it with the help of your electrician so that when your husband forgets the toilet seat, the light automatically goes off, signaling his oversight like the arrival of a silent police car. If only.

Auditory learners will need a verbal lesson, and this is where modern technology is truly a woman's best friend. Drop by your local Radio Shack and purchase a voice-activated mini-cassette recorder. Next record a gentle, loving reminder for your spouse, like "PUT THE SEAT DOWN, HONEY!!!" Attach the recorder to the underside of the commode with duct tape and place it on voice-activation mode, making sure the batteries are fresh. Then have yourself a glass of wine and wait for his scream. His backup, as one who learns through hearing, will need to be an alarm— preferably a loud one, such as a car alarm—which sounds when he tries to leave the bathroom. Warn the neighbors ahead of time.

For kinesthetic learners, things can be somewhat more expensive.

But remember what you are saving yourself from. You will need to purchase a European fanny washer and have a professional plumber install it in your commode. The result, which will be ever so effective, is that when your husband forgets to put down the seat, he gets a little squirt. Hopefully, he will not think this is refreshing.

Backup strategy for the kinesthetic learner involves a few wires on the bathroom door that deliver just the mildest of electrical volts. Nothing dangerous, mind you, just enough to remind him to turn around and complete the job—a bit like those shocks we got as a kid when we put our fingers in an outlet.

Follow these steps, and before long, darlin', you'll not only be thanking me, but your husband will be the one reminding you to PUT THE SEAT DOWN, HONEY!!!

The Air That I Breathe

It is with great regret—and no small amount of distaste—that I find myself compelled to raise this embarrassing subject. It is a truly terrible topic, and one that no Southern Girl should ever be required to discuss, much less live with. But discuss it we must. For, tragically, this issue is one of the darkest secrets that exist about marriage, and if I did not reveal it to you, I would not be worthy of my Southern Girl title.

The subject in question is male flatulence—or, simply put, the disgusting, unending and unbelievably revolting gas your husband will suddenly be capable of manufacturing after you have walked down the aisle.

Those of you with brothers will understand. After all, you grew up breathing the Pigpen-like vapors that followed them around. But the rest of you will have great difficulty believing what I am about to disclose. Frankly, I have difficulty believing it myself. After all, our very prim and proper Southern mother raised us to believe that bodily functions took place in one room and one room only. They did not take place in the kitchen, while you were enjoying a glass of wine. They did not take place during dinner, with company present. And they certainly did not take place in front of an air-conditioning vent as I nestled into bed, ready for romance.

Bodily functions, I was taught, took place on the commode, in the bathroom, with the door closed and the fan on full-blast. It is with this established mind-set that I met, dated and married my husband. And he is a wonderful man. But, oh, what a tangled web men weave when first they practice to pass gas.

Flatulence—like so many other conjugal secrets you would never conceive of—is an everyday reality with husbands. For many a married woman, it is an hour-by-hour struggle that can only be survived through great prayer (and extremely expensive air freshener). Without a doubt, it is the reason that Southern Girls wear so much perfume: to neutralize the odors of their husbands.

The truth of the matter is that everything you have ever hoped, everything you have ever heard, everything you have ever imagined about male flatulence—and, in particular, the so-called lack thereof—is a reprehensible fabrication. It is a lie that has been strategically perpetrated against the unwed female masses with one goal, and one goal only: the perpetuation of the human species. Because, believe me, dear Southern Girl, if brides had even the slightest idea how horrible their olfactory lives were about to become, the human race would go extinct in less time than it takes to say "aromatherapy."

But I am here to raise the banner of female awareness, and I intend to set the record straight. After much agony, many arguments and countless trips outside for fresh air, I am forced to tell you the tragic truth, and here it is: The real reason dogs are called "man's best friend" is that, since the beginning of time, men have been blaming these poor animals for their toots.[24]

It is not a subject you will hear about from Matt Lauer or Anderson Cooper. It is not something you will discuss in premarital counseling. Nor will you read about it in any marriage manual. In fact, if my gut feeling is correct, male flatulence may well be the best-kept secret in America. The reason for this is simple. The very survival of the male sex (life) depends upon it.

There is hope on the horizon, however. The latest research comes out of England, and focuses on "the foul smell of dog flatulence." Researchers from the Waltham Center for Pet Nutrition in Leicestershire, England, recently placed eight dogs—a golden retriever, five Labrador retrievers, and two English mastiffs—into outfits with a perforated tube and a pump containing a sensor that measured the amount of sulfide emitted by the animals. Then they fed the dogs special treats containing activated charcoal, zinc acetate and an extract of the yucca plant.[25]

The researchers concluded that, while the treats had no effect on how often the dogs were flatulent, they significantly reduced the amount of hydrogen sulfide and sharply reduced their unpleasantness. Translation: The dogs still tooted[26] a lot, but their toots didn't cause anyone to keel over.

Now what I would like to know is, why did they pick those particular breeds of dogs? What other scientific research on gas passing and dog breeds have we been missing? Is there secret, unreleased research that proves that a Labrador breaks wind five times more frequently—or more powerfully—than, say, a poodle? Maybe the president knows this, but is keeping it under wraps

---

[24]Like many Southern Girls, I loathe the hideous word that begins with the letter "f" and refuse to use it. Instead, we say "toots," "poots" or even "fluffs."

[25]Ummm. Special. Pass the charcoal, please.

[26]As with "tee-tee," this word can be used as both a noun and a verb.

so all of his corporate pals can make money from the findings. I can see it now: a run on poodles all across America. Poodle breeders— the new dot-com millionaires.

The second thing I would like to know is how much more frequently do these breeds experience sulfide emissions? How much more powerfully? And what sort of instrument is being used to measure this data? A tootometer?

Okay, before I get the animal activists sending me mail, let me state that I am a dog fanatic. I've had dogs all my life, and they have always slept in my bed, as a matter of fact. Under the covers. So I know what it means to live with dog toots (which, be forewarned, tend to multiply exponentially after consumption of turkey). It's a reason, if ever there was one, to love cats. And my dog, Gordon, certainly had a problem in this area. However, I am not at all sure that it is because Gordon is a dog that he had this affliction. While an overwhelming number of dogs do seem to suffer from flatulence, upon closer inspection of the issue, one will actually conclude that the problem is related to a very different characteristic of the dogs—a characteristic that is shared with many other species on the planet. That characteristic would be that the dogs are male.[27]

Results of Scientific Study Conducted by the Southern Girls Institute

Average number of poots per hour emitted by a woman: 1
(usually in the privacy of her bathroom)
Average number of poots per hour emitted by a man: 467
(usually in a confined space such as an elevator or car)

---

[27]My own personal conclusion, drawn from years of research.

Now, girls, I have done my research. I have observed my husband, father, stepfather, father-in-law and a bevy of uncles, half brothers, stepbrothers, cousins, friends and male colleagues in action. Moreover, I have used my own personal tootometer (covert action, of course) to accurately measure their emissions over the years, and my final calculations are as follows: For every poot emitted by a woman, typically in the privacy of her own bathroom, four hundred sixty-seven are emitted by a man—usually in a confined space such as an elevator or a car. Having been married for a decade, I have also developed the innate ability to instantly localize the origin of a silent-but-deadly one emitted in my presence. Being a polite, discreet and understated Southern Girl, I naturally do not bring this to the emitter's attention. Unless, of course, that emitter is my husband, in which case I hold my nose, make barfing sounds and yell, "Gross!" while running out of the room as fast as I can.

So, although I am not a scientist by training, my empirical data would lead me to believe that the researchers have been studying the wrong subjects. I think the experts should focus on something that will really get the economy back on track—namely, what sort of treats we can feed men so that their flatulence is significantly reduced. Say, to a dozen or so per hour.

In the meantime, does anyone know where I might get one of those suits for my husband?

FIVE

Men and Food:
Help Me, Rhonda

In the beginning, God said, "Let there be food." And there was food. God saw that the food was good. Man saw that the food was good. Woman came and cooked the food. And man was happy.

But woman grew tired—tired of planning, buying, hauling, storing, preparing and cooking the food. All the time, from the beginning of time. But there was nothing woman could do, because man's Mama had drilled man in the art of Learned Helplessness. She had cooked and cleaned and slaved for man all of his life so that man believed he was incapable of even the most basic of tasks. And God looked at man, in his state of Learned Helplessness. And it was not good.

Honey, Learned Helplessness began long before the foundations of the Earth, and long before your husband was born. Tragically, all men are afflicted with it, at least to a certain degree. So,
until you train your husband out of it, Learned Helplessness will
drive you stark raving mad.

This is the way it works, otherwise known as a Day in the Life
of a Hungry Husband.

It's Saturday morning and you have just spent two hours grocery
shopping for the week. Your husband has been out jogging. Which is
fine, because you don't let him do the shopping. The last time you
sent him for a can of pineapple, he came home with a bag of blueberries. Which meant that the Junior League did not enjoy the upside-
down cake that you'd promised them for their annual bake sale.

You return from the grocery store, look around for your husband and sigh when you hear the shower running. Because you
don't want the mahimahi to go bad, you lug in the packages and
unpack them. You tried letting him put away the groceries once,
too, but two days later, you found an open jar of Miracle Whip in
the pantry, tomatoes in the refrigerator and yogurt in the freezer.
His excuse? He "didn't know where they went."

Now it's past noon and you're starving. So you make yourself
a roast-beef sandwich, open a Diet Coke and settle onto the sofa
with your new book, which you've been dying to read for weeks.
Your husband comes down the stairs. "Did you make me one?" he
says, salivating over your lunch.

"No," you murmur, chuckling over your book. "You were in
the shower."

Your husband looks around the room as if somehow food
might miraculously appear on a silver platter, flying in the air to
greet him. Which it usually does—thanks to you. But your book
is too funny to put down.

"I'm hungry," he says, with just a hint of a whine.

You raise your eyes from the book for three seconds. "Well, make yourself a sandwich. I left the bread on the counter. Roast beef in the fridge."

"Okay."

You go back to reading, thinking the matter is solved. Sadly, your torment has only begun.

"What should I put on the sandwich?" he says, leaning into the refrigerator like a *Price Is Right* contestant pondering his options. You don't hear him. You're too engrossed with your book, which is hysterical.

"Honey?"

"Ummmm."

"What should I put on my sandwich?" he says, a note of anxiety creeping into his voice.

"Whatever you want."

Silence.

"Do we have any meat?"

You look up from your book.

Do you have any meat? Is he kidding? Of course you have meat! You gave up being a vegetarian—everything except bacon, of course—for him. You have meat in every variety on the planet: white, red, dark, light. You have so much meat in that refrigerator, you could open your own butcher business. Besides, you just told him there was roast beef in the fridge.

With the greatest of restraint, you force your voice to sound normal. "There's roast beef in the drawer," you repeat, going back to your book.

He nods, turns back to the refrigerator.

Silence. More silence. Still more silence.

You've now stopped reading because you know what's coming,

yet you hope—you dream!—that you are only imagining what he is about to ask. You are not.

"Uh, honey? What drawer would that be?"

You sigh. A long, protracted sigh that would communicate to anyone with a shred of emotional intelligence that the line is about to be crossed.

"The deli-and-cheese drawer," you answer.

"The big one at the bottom?"

You clench your teeth. "No," you say, with the patience of the turkey at a turkey shoot. After all, you've been sharing this refrigerator for the better part of a year now. "Notice the green stuff? That's the vegetable drawer. The deli-and-cheese drawer is the small one, in the middle."

"Ah," he says happily, sliding out the drawer and rustling the plastic on the deli bag. "I see it."

You go back to your book, convinced the matter is finally resolved.

"Do we have any mustard?" he says after another minute.

"Yes," you say, trying not to hiss.

"Where is it?'

You can't resist. "Where it always is!"

Silence. Give him credit now. This is a tricky one.

"Do you mean . . . the cabinet?" he says, like the kid about to win the national spelling bee.

You take another long breath. "The door of the refrigerator," you mutter. You pick up your book, but so sure are you that his next question is around the corner, you cannot even focus.

"Uh, honey. I don't see it."

"It's on the door! Third shelf from the top! Next to the mayonnaise and the salad dressings! Right above the biscuit rolls!"

More silence.

You've given up on the book. At this point, you're just skimming the words, not seeing anything—except red. Because you know what's coming. The four most dreaded words in the wife's universe. And here they are, right on cue.

"Can you help me?"

At this point, following in the footsteps of trillions of women the world over, you get up and grab the mustard—which of course was in front of him all along—and proceed to throw the sandwich together.

"Thanks," he says happily, diving into it a few minutes later. "So what do you want to do this afternoon?"

Learned Helplessness triumphs again.

Here's a great recipe for those times when you're sick in bed and your husband needs to make you a little something to eat. Enjoy!

Cinnamon Toast à la Husband

1. Take one piece of bread and put on counter.
2. Look for butter for three seconds, then ask wife where you can find it.
3. Repeat step 2.
4. Repeat step 2.
5. Finally discover butter, exactly where wife said it was. Cut off one big glob and put in the middle of bread. Do not spread any butter on the rest of the bread.

6. Take one tablespoon of sugar and dump onto glob of butter in center of bread.
7. Look for cinnamon for three seconds, then ask wife where you can find it.
8. Repeat step 7.
9. Repeat step 7.
10. Say, "Aha!" when wife gets out of bed and hands you cinnamon.
11. Pour one tablespoon of cinnamon onto central glob of butter and sugar.
12. Put in toaster oven on Broil.
13. Go to bathroom, read newspaper, wonder why smoke alarm is going off.
14. Turn off smoke alarm, open front and back doors of house to air out smoke.
15. Extract burned toast from toaster oven and scrape off burned covering.
16. Serve to wife in bed.

Hungry like the Wolf

When I met my husband, I had recently taken a series of classes at Le Cordon Bleu cooking school in London. I was, therefore, I must confess, somewhat more than impressed with my own personal culinary abilities. I made dough from scratch, transforming it into quiche, fruit pies, breads and scones. I marinated fish, steaks, chicken and lamb. I even perfected the art of homemade pasta.

"You made this yourself?" Mark would say, smearing strawberry-rhubarb jam on a steaming biscuit. "Is that possible?"

"It's a cinch," I would answer—and it is. Really. Here, I'll show you.

Annabelle's Strawberry-Rhubarb Jam

2½ lbs strawberries
2½ lbs rhubarb
5 lbs sugar
2 lemons (squeezed)

1. Wash all your fruit.
2. Cut off the tops of the strawberries, then cut them in half (quarters if they are really big).
3. Dump them all into a large pot on the stove and turn to medium-low.
4. Pour the sugar on top but don't mess with it. Don't even stir it. Just leave it alone till your sugar starts to melt.
5. Meanwhile, cut up your rhubarb in tiny little pieces. Give the strawberry-sugar mix a few stirs, add the lemon juice, then throw in all the rhubarb.
6. Stir again, then leave for at least three hours, stirring occasionally to make sure it's not sticking. Don't let it overflow, or you'll have a huge mess.
7. You'll know it's ready when it's almost as thick as you want it (it'll thicken more after it cools, so don't let it overcook).
8. Let cool, then ladle into some of those cute little jam jars you get at the grocery store (in twelve packs). Make sure

you wash the jars first, in the dishwasher, then fill them up not quite to the top.

9. Add the lids, but not very tight, and turn all the jars upside down on your counter (which seals).

10. A few hours later, turn 'em right side up and give the lids a final twist. Add pretty labels and, voilà, a year's supply of homemade jam. Or add a package of scones and a pretty bow, and use them for hostess gifts.

Jam is not the only trick I mastered. I whipped up a fresh hollandaise sauce for asparagus and a béarnaise for beef. I invented a creamy version of beef stroganoff that is sure to put five pounds on you in one sitting. I served bouillabaisse with rouille. I even made macaroni and cheese from scratch—which, I later learned, was not always a good thing (see the chapter on conflict resolution). I pulled it all together at six-course dinner parties. To my surprise, some of our friends were actually too intimidated to reciprocate—not exactly a strategy for energizing your social life. Oh, I was quite the little superstar of our six-foot kitchen.

Before me, Mark had lived a contented existence on meals composed largely of frozen food made edible thanks to the invention of the microwave. One evening, he invited me over for dinner. I watched, confused, as he grabbed a bag of frozen peas and another of frozen shrimp from the freezer. He then proceeded—and I am not making this up—to poor a pile of peas and a pile of shrimp onto two plastic plates.

I stood in the doorway of the kitchen, convinced that he was making food for the dog, as he placed one plate, then another, in the microwave. Finally, with a flourish, he set them on the dining room table with two forks, two paper towels and a jar of soy sauce. Then, gentleman that he was, he sat down and waited for me to join him.

My dilemma was twofold. First of all, Southern Girls are taught never to refuse hospitality, no matter how tacky that hospitality might be. Second, this man was cute—very cute. And he was the smartest guy I'd ever met—even if he did need to learn how to pull out a woman's chair. (He was, after all, a Yankee.) Still marriage material, despite his obvious confusion between edible and inedible. So without hesitation, I sat down to eat. We were married ten months later.

At the wedding, I discovered where Mark had learned his "cooking techniques" when my mother-in-law (see, everything eventually goes back to their mamas) gave her speech. "Honey," she said, "when it comes to cooking, you don't have to worry. My gift to you is that I have set the bar low—real low!" She then told a story about how Mark once said, with a look of adoration across his little face, "Mom, you make the best jello."

Boy, she wasn't kidding. When I married Mark, he thought Betty Crocker was home cooking. In fact, one of his favorite meals was Kraft Macaroni & Cheese from a box. It was a great setup. And, naturally, I had to go and ruin it.

I am not sure I was so much wooing Mark as I was showing off, but my culinary act began early on in our relationship, long before the proposal. On our first date, before we went to the theater, I impressed him with my beef stroganoff—mushrooms, caramelized onions and burgundy wine in a cream sauce over pasta. For my next performance, I marinated pork (which I had hitherto shunned for fish) in a citrus-lime sauce, before handing it over to be grilled. The appetizers were prunes wrapped in seared bacon and crackers smeared with baked garlic. Dessert? Apple pie à la mode, with my special crumble topping. Well, I must have been doing something right. He married me, which

I saw as further opportunity to spoil that man rotten with my cooking.

To my shock, however, about six months after the wedding, Mark started complaining that we didn't have any canned food. Yes, you heard me right. All my creative cooking, and the man wanted canned food. He just wouldn't let up about it, either. I felt like I was stuck in that scene from *Forrest Gump*, when Bubba talks about all the different ways you can cook shrimp. Canned beans, canned corn, canned peas, canned soup—all I heard was what Mark wanted in a can, and how I refused to buy it.

Well, let's just say that by then I had wisened up just a bit about the reality of cooking several meals a day, and it dawned on me. Why in tarnation was I trying to convince a man that he did not want to eat canned food, when people all over the world did just that—and lived to tell the tale? I mean, here he was offering me a mini-vacation every single day of my life, and I was trying to talk him out of it! Was I a lunatic? Definitely! A newlywed lunatic.

Having thus received my enlightenment, I drove straight to a warehouse store and stocked up on everything Mark had asked for. I bought six cases of canned food and came straight home, ready to enjoy some time off from all the meal preparation. Alas, it was not to be. Mark took one bite of his canned peas and pronounced them "bland." I was tempted to say, "I told you so!" Only I was too busy kicking myself.

I have no one to blame but myself, of course. I take full responsibility for introducing my husband to seasonal fruit and vegetables. I am at fault for teaching him to enjoy fresh fish, quail and foie gras, which he had never even heard of before he met me. I am just as guilty for introducing him to fresh-squeezed orange juice, which, with its hefty price tag and time-consuming work, is now the bane of my existence.

You see, during those early months of marriage, when I was

basking in the satisfied grunts of my new husband and feeling oh so pleased with my little cooking self, I was creating a monster. A gourmet monster who knew just how good grilled-cheese sandwiches could be if they were made with Brie and cranberry sauce and who wasn't about to go back to Velveeta, much less those squares euphemistically called "American cheese," no, sirree, Bob. Like a lamb leading herself to the slaughter, I had trained my husband's palate for the finer food in life, and let me tell you, after drinking Château Lafitte, there ain't a man on God's green Earth who's going back to Piggly-Wiggly wine-in-a-box.

Mark now raises his eyebrows (much like I used to, I'm afraid) at the sight of frozen food, as if the mere sight of it is offensive. He knows the difference between brownies from a mix and those made from cocoa. He won't touch soup from a can, and will only concede to canned tuna (spiced up, of course) if he is very hungry indeed—and if no female is around to prepare something better. But will he actually cook one of those gourmet dishes? No, darlin'. Not a chance in the world. Connoisseur though he may be, my husband remains very much a man. A man with a double PhD in the art of Learned Helplessness, as a matter of fact.

So beware, Girls. Be very, very aware. I have learned the hard way that my mother-in-law was right. She knew exactly what to do when it comes to cooking for men. She knew to leave the bar low.

How Low Can You Go

Unlike most mothers-in-law—especially your average Southern mother-in-law—mine did not spoil her son rotten. She did not cultivate the terrain for his future wife to experience a lifetime of failure in the kitchen. And for that, I say praise God, hallelujah and thank you, Donna. In fact, unless you count frozen dinners (which Mark actually heated himself), my mother-in-law rarely even cooked. She kept the bar so low that Mark actually had a running joke about it.

"Want to know what my mom makes best?" he'd say, then pause a beat before saying, "Reservations."

This was extremely helpful for me, because it meant that Mark's expectations were rock-bottom when it came to food. And I do mean rock-bottom—as in peas, shrimp and soy sauce. Unfortunately, this is not the case with other men, especially Southern Boys, who are used to being served three meals a day, and who can probably name two or three favorite dishes that "Mama always makes." Try though you might, however, you will never replicate those dishes. They will always be just a little off, probably because of that secret ingredient your mother-in-law "forgot" to include when she gave you the recipe. Therefore, in his eyes, Mama was, is and forever more shall be Queen of the Lemon Meringue Pie.

The solution? Do nothing. Not only is this one less thing your husband will expect you to cook, but you'll also win a few brownie points (no pun intended) with his mother by graciously accepting defeat. Meantime, enjoy the pie, even if you have to choke it down. Remember, you're out to win the war, not these flaky battles.

Keeping the bar low, when it comes to food, is a lifelong commitment. Like most goals, it involves great dedication and perseverance. You must also be constantly on the prowl for those who would wreck the work that you have so carefully created, by demonstrating that gourmet food at home is actually possible. This means, essentially, avoiding people your own age who know how to cook. Fortunately, this will not be very difficult.

The first thing to remember, when it comes to feeding men, is that unlike women, most men eat to live—not live to eat. Also, unless it's baseball stats, men have little long-term memory.[28] Therefore, the longer he's away from Mama, the less likely it is that your husband will remember her cooking—with the exception of one or two things (like her lemon meringue pie). Second, frozen burgers and fries are a grown man's Happy Meal. Serve them whenever you can. Third, men don't care how tasty their chicken soup is. They just want the hunger pains to go away. And they are not going to distinguish between store-bought muffins and the warm blueberry ones that kept you up past midnight. If they're like my husband—who won't recognize food unless it's on a plate in front of him, with a neon arrow pointing toward it and a voice shouting, "Eat!"—they might even let those muffins grow moldy. After all, how could a man be expected to notice fresh baked blueberry muffins on a raised glass cake plate, in the middle of the counter, right where they pour their coffee every morning?

With these principles in mind, we now move to the food rules of marriage. By adhering to them, you will be able to satisfy your husband's ongoing need for food every day, while saving yourself from certain insanity. I call them "The Home Depot Newlywed Kitchen Rules," in honor of that great Atlanta institution, founded by men.

The Home Depot Newlywed Kitchen Rules

1. MAINTAIN QUALITY CONTROL OVER YOUR STOCK: NEVER DELEGATE THE GROCERY SHOPPING.

Your groceries and staples are like the stock at a very good store. They keep you in business, day in and day out, and make your work

---

[28]Although this poses a problem in the gift department, it will seriously play in your favor when the credit-card bills arrive.

flow smoothly. When you need some dried basil, it's in the cabinet. Honey mustard is in the fridge, along with everything else you need for a decent sandwich. But in order for that to happen, you need to maintain quality control over everything in your kitchen. You prefer certain brands and specific sizes—something that might seem obvious at first, but which is bound to confuse your husband. Thus the rule: Never delegate the grocery shopping to him.

To the newlywed bride, this will no doubt seem antiquated. After all, men can help with other chores (at least in theory), so why not the grocery shopping? Well, at the risk of you thinking I'm a Stepford wife, I must disillusion you. First of all, never in the history of the world has there been a nongay man who has actually enjoyed going to the grocery store, much less spending the kind of time in one that it takes to get your weekly shopping done. For reasons that anthropologists have yet to ascertain, grocery stores give grown men hives and cause them to hyperventilate. And if you don't believe me, just take your husband to one, hang around for the time that it takes the Muzak version of "Feelings" to finish and just watch him fall apart.

Even if you can convince him to take on the weekly (daily) task of grocery shopping, you'll have to overcome some serious hurdles. First of all, he'll have no clue what to buy, which means that you'll need to give him a detailed list each time. Then, assuming he remembers to take that list—which is a big assumption— good luck in getting him to get more than a tenth of the items on it. After all, finding a pair of clean socks in a drawer full of 'em is a problem for most men. Locating bread machine yeast is like discovering the Ark of the Covenant.

Then there's the Confusion Factor. Men see grocery stores as perplexing mysteries of the universe. Of course, if I'd been avoiding 'em all my life, they might be a little confusing for me, too. Still, it's not as if going to the grocery store flips my skirt. Yes, I've made friends with half the checkout gals and know all the deli workers by name, but that's because I spend so much dang time there. What else am I going to do when I see the same people, day after day, week after week? It's the Southern way. But not the Yankee way, let me tell you. No, ma'am. Mark doesn't even look at cashiers, much less get into a conversation about their kids, grandkids and great-uncle's friend's hernia. Shocking, isn't it?

Now my Chatty Cathy ways don't mean—as any good Southerner will know—that I enjoy spending my free time pushing a buggy[29] up and down the aisles of a grocery store. It's just one of those things in life that needs to be done—and so far, I haven't met more than a few men who are both willing and capable of doing it. I've therefore learned to think of grocery stores as a necessary part of life—kinda like bathrooms and exercise. You just do it.

Easy-to-Confuse Grocery Store Items for Husbands

- No-fat milk, low-fat milk, whole milk ("What color is the carton?")
- Sour cream and cream cheese ("What's the difference again?")
- Strawberries, raspberries, blueberries and blackberries ("They all looked the same to me.")
- Band-Aids and Bain de Soleil ("Well, they were right beside each other on the shelf.")
- Butter and Butterfingers ("Um, I'll just eat the Butterfingers, then.")

---

[29]Southern for "grocery cart."

The problem is that even armed with a list, men will have great difficulty figuring out what it says. If they can read your handwriting (always the front-line defense for items they can't find), they will still confuse Cool Whip with Kool-Aid, Butterfingers with I Can't Believe It's Not Butter, and sour cream with cream cheese. So sending them to the grocery store, assuming all the stars are aligned and Jesus is on his way back, is a bit like hitting the I'M FEELING LUCKY button for a Google search. You just never know what you might get. Which is not to say it won't be something interesting and unique—you just won't be able to use it in the pound cake you were making for his mother's birthday party, which starts in an hour.

The other problem with men and grocery shopping is that they tend to be like teenagers let loose in the mall with a credit card. Comparison shopping? Forget it. Store brands? Not a chance. The things he does manage to buy will be the most expensive in the store. Half of the items on your list will be missing, but never fear, he'll bring home a lifetime supply of batteries, extension cords and lightbulbs, not to mention some interesting sausages that you never knew he liked—and which he won't like after you cook them. Too bad they were so expensive. And hey, honey, did you see these steaks I picked up? I was thinking that we could cook them for the block party tonight. Organic, grass-fed Angus rib eyes, at $24.99 a pound.

Finally, all this is compounded by the fact that he doesn't want to be there in the first place, so he will be rushing up and down the aisles as fast as he can, trying to get out. And, in so doing, it can be mighty easy to confuse an extra-large can of Crisco, which has a picture of a lovely baked chicken on the label, with an actual baked chicken. Just ask the Southern Girl whose husband proudly brought home the tub of lard, thinking they could eat the fowl within that night for dinner.

As I type, I am still shaking my head at my husband and father-in-law, who have just returned from Trader Joe's, a store that I have fallen in love with.[30] Mark and his daddy had promised to buy five items for me that you can only get at Trader Joe's. To make things easy—and despite the fact that the store is tiny—I wrote down the section for each item, as in *Crumbled Danish blue cheese: refrigerated section, right side of store*. Then, just in case, I went over the list with my father-in-law, item by item. After all, the store is an hour away, and I wanted to make sure they didn't mess this one up.

Girl, please. When those two got home, they put the groceries on the counter (for me to put away) and you'd 'a thought they just scaled Stone Mountain in an ice storm, they were so proud. However, they'd managed only to get one thing right on the list. Forgetting our little review session, my father-in-law (who just happens to have a PhD and has invented some forty name-brand household items) said that he "couldn't read my handwriting." When I asked my husband why he had confused pumpkin puree with pumpkin pie spice, he said, "I asked for pumpkin pie spice, but the guy in the store directed me to this. Is there a difference?"

Well, let's see. During our discussion, before you left, I did explain that pumpkin pie spice was a "spice" and pointed to all the spice bottles in the cabinet, just to make sure you had a visual in mind, before heading off to the wilds of the grocery store. But that's okay. We'll just save the pumpkin for next year.

So, like most seasoned wives, you will probably discover that it's far easier—and quicker and cheaper—to do all the grocery shopping yourself. You will probably want to put away the food, too. After all, it's highly unlikely that you'd ever think to look in the fridge for that box of pasta or the china cabinet for your soy sauce. Don't

[30]You want fresh, organic and cheap—go to Trader Joe's, which will hopefully open some stores in the deep South very soon. Please, y'all!

laugh. I found an entire pound of butter in my pantry just last week. On the top shelf, too. Honest.

If he balks—and I can't imagine that he will—ask him to look at it like this: He is the customer, your kitchen is Home Depot, you are the Home Depot supplier. Does he really want to run all over town looking for lumber, nails and a saw when you can have them right at the tip of his fingers? Besides, this is where his job comes in—building his meal.

2. FOR EVERY PROFESSIONAL JOB, COME TWO
   DO-IT-YOURSELFERS: YOU MAKE DINNER,
   BUT HE'S ON HIS OWN FOR BREAKFAST
   AND LUNCH.

Unless you are an unemployed, stay-at-home wife with nothing but time on your hands—or a gourmet chef who loves to be in the kitchen—your husband will need to be trained to make his own breakfasts and lunches. And you, honey, must resist all temptation to do it for him, except in very special circumstances. You may think this will be a breeze, especially if you don't know how to cook. But even if you've never done more than toast a bagel, wedding bells have a way of making you fantasize about waffles and smoked-salmon scrambled eggs—not to mention that look on his face when you serve them.

Remember, however, that no matter how adorable you look in your Pottery Barn apron, marriage is a training ground. Everything you do is part of that training—especially when it is related to food. And once you start down a certain road, there is no going back. Besides, the only look on his face when you serve him his meal is going to be determination—to eat it as fast as possible and get back to the game. It's not like he's going to be transformed into a cheerleader for your cooking, no matter how good it is. Men are minimalists at best when it comes to gratitude, honey.

But again, Home Depot thinking to the rescue. You love and adore your husband, which is why you stock the kitchen with food every week, just like the Home Depot suppliers stock those warehouses. Every possible item he could dream of is there, right before his very eyes, waiting for him to select. All for him! Okay, so maybe you don't have forty thousand items like they do, but you certainly have more than your husband—and maybe you—will ever use.[31]

In addition to stocking his favorite "store" with food, you also show your love for your new husband by making dinner every single night—kind of like Home Depot's At-Home Services, which sends contractors to your house to take care of the more challenging tasks. One hot meal a day at home—that's what he's going to get! Isn't that great? Aren't you wonderful? Isn't he glad he married you? Just think how much better this is than his bachelor days, when he had to do all that by himself. It's all in the presentation, girls. If ever there was time to hone your sales pitch, this is it.

You may find it necessary to debunk some of his more unrealistic expectations, prior to implementing this strategy. After all, if he's like most men, he came into your union expecting a constant food- and sex-a-thon. And whether or not you are responsible for creating the food expectation, as I certainly was, this is your chance to wipe it out. (The sex, we'll get to later.)

For your husband to understand that he is responsible for two meals a day, you must first help him understand that the concept of three home-cooked meals a day—at least by you, anyway—is out of the question. It never existed. It died before it began. It was, tragically, a figment of his imagination. It's over, so get over it.

[31] I've always believed that a little extra food in the pantry makes a woman feel good, ya know?

If he argues, tell him that you were actually thinking that he'd be cooking for you after you got married. When the horror crosses his face, say, "Well . . . all right. I guess I'd be willing to cook one meal a day—dinner. But you're responsible for the other two meals." This is called "bait and switch," and it works very well and makes lots of money for large corporations.

If he really bucks, remind him that this is a 33 percent improvement rate over his bachelor days. Compare that to the old interest rate at the bank! Remind him further that you're doing the grocery shopping, which makes it an even better deal. If he still complains, tell him—with great excitement in your voice—that it will be just like going to Home Depot. At first, he may feel overwhelmed with choices and decisions, but when he gets his bearings, he'll find whatever he needs to get the job done. Soon, he will discover that preparing mini-meals for himself will give him a tremendous sense of accomplishment. Remind him of the time that he buttered his own toast. Be very affirming, but do not give in to any of his pleas, no matter how guilty they make you feel. Remember, he's had years of practice making Mama feel guilty. He's an expert.

If he's truly clueless—as in his mama not only cooked all of his meals during high school but never let him lift a finger during college either, or perhaps a previous girlfriend succumbed to Learned Helplessness one too many times as well—you will need to do further legwork before this plan can kick into action.

3. HE CAN DO IT. YOU CAN HELP.
   BUT NOT TOO MUCH.

Home Depot has a wonderful motto, which I just adore, and which makes me feel incredibly empowered whenever I hear it. "You can do it," they say, with a nice musical jingle. "We can help." When it comes to food, this is just the motto your husband needs to hear. You'll show him, but he's going to do those two meals himself, even if it's just unwrapping a granola bar or heating up a Hungry Man.

You will need to make a map—a kitchen map. It needn't be a fancy one—no Lewis and Clark stuff. In fact, if you put too much detail on this map, your husband will get lost. Remember, he's not used to asking or following directions, unless they're on the football field. We're talking basic survival here. The trick is to give him just enough information to successfully pour a bowl of cereal or—and this can be tricky, but he'll soon get the hang of it— actually make himself a sandwich. Use the word "build," if you can, as in "build a sandwich." It has a nice, masculine ring to it.

Combating Learned Helplessness in the Kitchen

1. Draw a kitchen map that shows the strategic locations of key items in your cabinets: plates, glasses, utensils, bread, canned tuna and potato chips.
2. Draw a refrigerator map with the location of basic male survival items: milk, orange juice, deli meats, hot dogs, cheese, lettuce, condiments and pickles.
3. Place both maps on refrigerator door at eye level.
4. Point out the existence of these maps to your husband. Make sure he is paying attention.
5. Point out the existence again the next day, when he asks.
6. When husband still cannot find maps, three weeks later, start calling them "treasure maps." Offer a prize, if he finds them. Like dinner.

For your map, take a white piece of paper and draw an overhead design of your kitchen cabinets, including your sink, stove and fridge. Next with **BOLD RED LETTERS** indicate exactly where your husband can find the basic male pantry staples: bread, canned tuna and potato chips. Pictures, instead of words, are even better. Be creative. And don't forget to include a few pots and pans—actually, just one pot and one frying pan. You don't want to confuse him.

Next to your kitchen map, on the same piece of paper, you will also need to draw a refrigerator map—kind of like those little blow-up maps you get online for your final destination. Draw your map as if you are looking inside, with the shelves in front of you and the door on the side. Again, keep it simple. Concentrate on the basics: milk, orange juice, deli meats, cheese, lettuce, mustard/ketchup/mayo, dill pickles and hot dogs. Don't bother to indicate items that will never interest him, such as cilantro, diet butter and chardonnay, and be sure to indicate exactly what shelf each item is on. Numbering is good, too. You won't need to point out the beer or ice cream—men can always find those items, no matter how buried. And your Coke bottles should be right there on the counter, after you've opened them, or in the pantry—if you like carbonation, that is. But it wouldn't hurt to mention this, too. Remember my blueberry muffins.

Place both maps within plain view on the freezer door so that he can look at them as he opens the fridge and even take them with him when he moves around the kitchen. Then give him a little Home Depot how-to clinic. Show him the maps, show him the food, then show him how to use the two together. See? He can do it. Don't be surprised, however, when he asks you where the maps are the next day. It can take months—years, in some cases—for the average husband to remember that the maps are right there in front of him. You can always try calling them "treasure maps," though. After all, we're dealing with a Peter Pan, I-don't-want-to-grow-up issue, if ever there was one.

Also, it is probably worthwhile to make several blank copies of the refrigerator map, for times when you need to move food around, such as the holidays. Otherwise, you will be stuck answering questions all day long, which may tempt you to give in and make his meal. Do so at your own risk.

4. KEEP ALL PROJECTS SIMPLE.

When it comes to cooking, keeping the bar low means taking advantage of everything that this great country has to offer. Fortunately, thanks to America's gimme-right-now-and-make-it-snappy mentality, you can cook dinner for your husband every single night without ever having to wash, chop or cut. We are a nation of farmers and ranchers, and we produce everything from fruits, vegetables and dairy products to meat, chicken and fish. It's a wonderful cornucopia of plenty, and thank goodness giant corporations have transformed it all into frozen and prepackaged goods.

What this means is that all you need to know how to do is open bags and use your microwave. I've even seen cooking shows where entire meals are made from cans, and you'd never even know it. This is an art, in my opinion, that more women need to excel at. So save the signature dishes for the holidays and visits from Mama and Daddy, when you need to impress, and work on getting dinner on the table every night. As my grandmother used to say, "That's a full-time job."

Do not neglect the power of the casserole. I had all but forgotten about these until a Midwestern girlfriend kept inviting us over and serving them for dinner. After the second or third time,

I started to get a little offended. I mean, I didn't expect a gourmet meal (although I did make them for her when she and her husband came to visit), but how about something other than tuna casserole? Then it dawned on me. Casseroles! Maybe not for guests, but for husbands? Definitely! Why hadn't I thought of that?

As soon as I started making casseroles, Mark started gobbling them down. I had hit the mother lode. He even takes the leftovers for lunch now. As Cervantes, Spanish author of the classic *Don Quixote*, once said, "Hunger is the best sauce in the world."

Everyday Chicken Casserole

Here's an easy recipe that works well for everyday dinners. Your husband can take leftovers, or you can serve it again the next day, perhaps with a bowl of soup. For a lighter version, choose low-fat soups, cheese and sour cream.

16 oz. box of spiral pasta or noodles
4 boneless, skinless chicken breasts
10 oz. can cream of chicken soup
10 oz. can cream of mushroom soup
8 oz. bag of shredded sharp Cheddar cheese
8 oz. carton of sour cream
Plain croutons

1. Boil the chicken breasts in a deep frying pan, filled with water. Remove when cooked thoroughly, about five minutes. Chop into small pieces.

2. Boil the pasta and drain.
3. Combine all ingredients except croutons and stir well.
4. Place into large casserole dish (or two smaller ones) and add croutons on top.
5. Lightly coat croutons with butter spray.
6. Cover with tinfoil and bake at 350° F until bubbly.

The ideas are endless, when it comes to dinner, but simplicity reigns supreme. And your husband, if you are wise enough to keep him in the dark, will be blissfully unaware that there is anything else out there. Which leads me to my final rule.

5. DO YOUR RESEARCH WHEN IT COMES TO OUTSIDE CONTRACTORS: AVOID OTHER COUPLES WHO KNOW HOW TO COOK.

This is important, because if any of your friends knows how to cook, the bar will get raised—and your husband will get suspicious. How do you spot potential talent? The warning signs will all be located in their home. First, search for cookbooks. The further from the kitchen they are kept, the less likely they are to be used. Are they dusty? If so, you're safe. The same goes for cooking magazines like *Bon Appétit* and *Gourmet*, which will need to be very, very old.

Examine the kitchen for any gadgets that whisper "connoisseur." Items such as food processors, stand mixers and pasta makers will be of significant concern. A mini-blowtorch (used for crème brûlée) is a dead giveaway. Should you happen to spot a diploma from cooking school, you will need to evacuate the house as quickly as possible.

Warning Signs of
People with Culinary Talent

- Cookbooks with signs of use
- Recent copies of *Bon Appétit*, *Gourmet* or other cooking magazines
- Food processor, stand mixer, pasta maker, mini-blowtorch
- Diploma from cooking school
- Awards from cooking school

Although you will want to avoid these people like moldy cheese, you do not want to offend them when they invite you over to sample their culinary creations. Tempted though you will be, however, you must never accept, under any circumstances. The stakes are simply too great. The challenge will therefore be to maintain those friendships without ever eating at their table. This will be difficult, but fortunately, those who love to cook also love to eat, which means that they will enjoy dining out. Hopefully, the restaurant food will be far tastier than yours, which will lead your husband to assume that a "nonprofessional" could never produce such delights.

Congratulations. Mission accomplished.

SIX

Men and Their Idiosyncrasies: Funkytown

Ah, men. Is there anything sexier? Probably not, but, honey, let's be honest now. Is there anything more "different," either? Men may cry "PMS" (and certainly, there's a nasty reality lurking behind that little accusation), but as far as I'm concerned, if there's anything scarier than Eric Rudolph with a stick of dynamite, it's your husband's idiosyncrasies.

My newlywed trial by fire (one of them, anyway—let's not limit ourselves) took place in the bedroom. I'm not talking about sex now, which was and is wonderful—give or take the few messy details we all contend with. In this case, I am actually referring to sleeping. That is, the act of placing oneself into a reclining position on a bunch of metal coils next to another live human being, with just inches between you, and actually expecting to get more than five minutes of rest. Who invented the double bed, anyway?

Talking in Your Sleep

Before I married, I never understood couples like my grandparents who slept in separate bedrooms. Even if my grandfather did perform a soporific opera every night with his nose, I just knew that when I wed, I would spend every sleeping moment snuggled up to my husband, basking in the glow of our lovemaking and falling asleep with his arms wrapped around me. After all, that's why "spooning" was invented, right? The smaller the bed, the better.

Boy, talk about delusional.

Reality intruded, as it often does, during the honeymoon. On our third night in Hawaii, after an evening of lobster, champagne and romance, Mark rolled over about three a.m. and sat up, wide-awake. Cupping my face in both hands, with a look of utmost passion, he shouted, "Annabelle, I love you sooooo much!"

I melted. "Oh, honey. I love you, too." With that, we snuggled up and went back to sleep. What a sweet, sweet man. The next morning, I was still basking in the afterglow, but my dear husband had no recollection whatsoever of the amorous incident. Although somewhat surprised, I was nevertheless comforted by the thought that, while deep in slumber, my dear new husband was dreaming of me and our undying love. How romantic!

The next night I had another glimpse into Mark's subconscious. Sometime after two a.m., he shook me awake. "Annabelle! Wake up! Wake up!" he shouted. Being one of the lightest sleepers on the planet, I immediately sat up in bed. "What? What's wrong?" I shouted.

"Tell me you love me!" Mark said, as if commanding a platoon of soldiers to attack al-Qaeda terrorists.

"What?"

"Tell me you love me!"

"I love you, honey," I said, surprised. But the next morning, he had once again forgotten the incident. So when it happened a third night, I was not quite as enchanted. Besides, by then, I was also sleep deprived.

"Tell me you love me!" Mark ordered. I tried to ignore him, but he kept repeating the request until I woke up. I looked at my husband in the light of the moon. His eyes were closed and his words were thick.

"You're talking in your sleep, honey," I said.

"No!" he insisted, turning his head back and forth across the pillow. "Tell me you love me."

"Shhhh, you're not going to remember any of this in the morning. Go back to sleep."

"Tell me you love me!" he said, his voice beginning to slur. "Tell me!"

I sighed. "Okay. I love you."

Mark rolled over, settled down and started to go back to sleep. I heaved a sigh of relief and did the same, until suddenly I heard him say, "Now tell me again!"

These were the first of our sleep adventures. Since then, my husband has traveled many a mile and lived exotic exploits—all in his sleep. He's been chased by a wild boar. He's confronted a mafioso. He has preached—at the Vatican, I believe (I heard the entire sermon). While details of his escapades remain elusive, he is always good for a few mumbled, nonsensical but very funny words.

"Crinkle! Crinkle! Crinkle!" he once said, as I rustled a plastic bag at the foot of our bed. "No!" he shouted to an invisible colleague of, shall we say, stately proportions. "Don't sit in that chair!" Recently he mumbled, "I won't do it. I won't, I won't, I won't," no doubt referring to some hideous torture—like cooking himself a meal.

But these adventures pale next to the exploits of other husbands. One Southern Girl awoke late at night to see her husband frantically moving items around the room. When she asked what in Sam Hill he was doing, he strode over and pushed both of her arms above her head. He then insisted, in a sleep-addled voice, that she "hold the shelf" while he "nailed it to the wall." Then he proceeded to "do" just that—with an invisible hammer. Whenever she lowered her arms, even the slightest bit, he shouted and hoisted them up again. No amount of logic would dissuade her nocturnal carpenter from his task, and she couldn't wake him up. Eventually, he finished "the shelf" and climbed back into bed.

The next morning, when she complained about the incident and her aching arms, he denied everything. After trying in vain to convince him that he did, indeed, have an entirely separate nocturnal personality, she finally pulled out her trump card—the nightstand. There, lined up like Yankees ready to fire on Southern secessionists were dozens of objects from their bedroom and bathroom—everything from shoes and socks to perfume, lotion and jewelry.

Another Southern Girl is subject to her husband's nightly "trips" to the roof of the "hospital," where he helps unload injured "patients" from a whirring helicopter—all the while shouting orders at her.[32] Still another Southern Girl must endure the ecstatic moans of her husband, as he clutches and hugs a pillow every night. Not her, mind you—a pillow. And these are just the sleepwalkers and talkers. My sister's husband snores so loudly she has to

---

[32]This man does not, by the way, work in the medical profession.

wear earplugs every night. And my godmother must somehow drift off to sleep next to her husband's nasal noises, which sound like choking seagulls.

Night Moves

Also, call it human nature, but when it comes to sleeping, most men are thieves. Although Mark claims he has no knowledge of his nighttime forays onto my side of the bed, his eight-foot-long, hundred-pound leg just happens to fling itself, with alarming frequency, all the way across the mattress every night. As if that isn't enough, whenever I need to get up—or worse, while I happen to be in the middle of a wonderful dream—my husband's arm always seems to land on my chest. *Thunk!* And, oh, yes, he also loves to ball himself up in the covers and roll—roll—away from me, taking the sheets, the blanket and the quilt with him as he goes, leaving me completely uncovered in a room that feels like northern Virginia on a cold and frosty morn. Any attempt to move him, or recover the stolen covers, is doomed. First of all, he's a very deep sleeper (hence, the sleep talking). Second, it takes him at least an hour and three strong cups of coffee in the morning to decipher his own thoughts, much less verbal contact from another human. Which leaves me suffocating and freezing to death.

Now I have other methods, which usually involve poking him a lot. It's fairly effective. And, hey, it's not like he remembers anything that happens during the night, right? He's probably being prodded into an Iraqi prison cell by an AK-47-wielding terrorist.

What's a girl to do? Well, first of all, consider the underutilized idea of separate bedrooms. Before you scoff at the idea, hear me when I say that after more than a decade of conjugal bliss, I am here to tell you that sleeping separately is an underrated concept. After all, it's not like snoozing together is quality time, right? Just think about it: your own bed, your own pillows, your own covers and your own TV. You can eat in bed. Talk on the phone in bed. Do your toes in bed. And when you want your husband, he's right down the hall. Don't forget to install an intercom to beckon him. Because believe me, he will definitely come a-runnin' whenever you call.[33]

Remember, Scarlett and Rhett had separate bedrooms, and they were madly in love. Okay, so maybe that's not the best example, but once those babies start coming, someone's going to be on the sofa, anyway—and it better not be you.

Sleeping Options for Married Couples

- Separate bedrooms
- Separate beds
- California king-sized bed
- King-sized bed
- Dog bed

If rooms are an issue, consider a hotel-style bedroom—two double beds, right beside each other. The downside to this arrangement is that you'll still have to put up with his snoring, his sleep talking and his sleepwalking. You will also have to share the TV—unless you each buy one with headphones. And you'll have

---

[33]I have yet to resort to this strategy, except during postpartum periods, but I like the thought. A lot.

to look at his unmade bed every day, until you get him trained to make it.

On the other hand, separate beds mean that you'll have your own set of covers and pillows, and no twitching or bouncing to deal with. Those of you who have twitching or bouncing husbands know exactly what I am talking about, but for those who do not, allow me to explain. A twitching husband is one who appears to sleep peacefully but who, without warning, will regularly jerk and spasm as if undergoing electric-shock treatment. A bouncing husband, on the other hand, is one who forgets that he is no longer eight years old and who, upon entering the bed, throws himself in with the force of an Olympic jumper. The resulting undulations of the mattress, which will cause you to spill your water, drop your book and—if you're married to my husband—suffer from a severe case of whiplash, will have you wondering if you somehow mistakenly purchased a waterbed.

So separate beds. Think hard, y'all.

For those of you who have visions of nighttime snuggle plums still dancing in your head, I realize that these novel, visionary ideas may seem far-fetched, and will probably not sway you from the fantasy of bed sharing with your beloved. That's okay. Like my middle sister and I used to say to each other about our younger sister, when she dispensed parenting advice before having a baby: "We'll talk in a few years." Meantime, trust me when I tell you that, at the very least, you must get yourself a king-sized bed—preferably a California king. Yes, I know that in the Middle Ages entire families slept in beds the size of a twin, and without the slightest comfort of modern bedding, so what can it hurt to have two people—especially you two, who love each other so much—sharing one bed? Just remember that in the Middle Ages, people also drank copious amounts of wine every night for dinner, making it easier to sleep with a man whose snores could wake the dead. Which might be another idea, come to think of it.

So you need a big bed—and the bigger, the better. Even if you have to install mosquito netting and put the thing out on the sleeping porch, for lack of room, you will thank me someday. And if you must sleep in a queen-sized bed (less is truly unthinkable), then be sure to buy king-sized sheets and blankets so there's extra room when he starts grabbing. In some cases, you may need two sets of king-sized sheets and blankets. I also suggest that you purchase one of those oversized dog beds and put it next to his side of the bed. Because eventually, after you get fed up with his nighttime antics and are forced to do a little shoving, he's going to need a soft place to land.

I'd Like to Teach the World to Sing

Singing husbands are an interesting lot. While most tend to be private crooners who limit the expression of their budding talent to the shower, others prefer an audience. Unless your husband happens to sound like Barry White, this can be annoying. If, on the other hand, he would qualify as a reject from one of the early rounds of *American Idol*, it will be embarrassing as well. Worse still is the husband who not only sings like William Hung (a kid who's made a career out of sounding like he's being hung), but also believes he could take on Clay Aiken.[34] Exercising his vocal cords for you whenever possible, this husband is apt to bellow anything from "Because You Loved Me" and "Thriller" to "Ring My Bell," depending on his age.

[34]Actually, I was a Reuben fan myself.

It's My Party

Men's most annoying idiosyncrasies tend to be connected to their bodies. Actually, I take that back. Men are forever finding new and creative ways of annoying us, and I never cease to be amazed at their ingenuity in this arena—which is, now that I think of it, exactly why I wrote this book. So let's just say that strange and annoying personal habits are but one of the ways in which men excel at exasperating us, and leave it at that.

Wives must put up with everything from minor habits, like husbands obsessively flexing their muscles in the mirror, clipping their toenails in bed and cracking their knuckles, to more extreme versions of these oddities, like obsessively looking at their manhood in the mirror (do they think it's going to grow?), not clipping their toenails at all (ever been stabbed by one of those?) and cracking your knuckles. Don't laugh. I had a boyfriend who tried this on me once.

Some husbands spend far too much time in front of the mirror—shaving, popping zits, clipping nose hairs—then complain when we make them wait. Others rival beauty queens when it comes to hairstyling. Who invented hair gel for men, anyway? I'm told that when they get older, it gets even worse. Just look at Donald Trump.

Even more ubiquitous among men is the problem of nose picking, which appears to have reached epidemic proportions. Given its extreme popularity, in fact, I can't help but wonder what aspect of the male psyche this activity involves. It's as if man, in his quest to achieve alpha-male status, finds meaning within his nostrils. He is the superhero in search of the archenemy. As he wrestles the villain from his lair, he is annihilating evil's stronghold on society at large. This explains why, even when the task is impossible—and embarrassment a foregone conclusion—man is unstoppable in his mission. He cannot give up until he has won the Battle of the Booger.

Cat Scratch Fever

Women could write an entire book on the subject of men and scratching. Men scratch incessantly, and they scratch in public. They scratch when you're looking at them, when you're not looking at them and when they think you're not looking at them (but you are). They scratch in front of your mother. They scratch in front of their mothers—who should have stopped the business long ago, if you ask me. Men scratch, quite frankly, without regard to place, time, audience or event. And they do it in the most embarrassing manner possible.

The same thing can be said for rearranging. Men enjoy rearranging themselves, and they do it throughout the day. Now, while they scratch various parts of their bodies, they can only rearrange one particular area. Combine this with scratching (as they do), and you've got yourself a problem. Given most men's lack of reticence and seemingly unstoppable urge in this area, it can be quite embarrassing for new wives. Some men do it in a way that they consider "discreet." But even a gentleman's definition of discreet has nothing—I repeat, nothing—to do with how a woman would define that word, and discreet for one man is often ostentatious to another. The bottom line is that no matter how subtle your husband may think he is being, there really is no way to touch your genitals in public without people noticing, now, is there?

A bigger problem is that many men believe it is their God-given right to scratch and rearrange. Of course, one might assume that God gave men this right, but God gave us mouths, too. And while some men think it's okay to say whatever they want, whenever they want—just like scratching—we know just how wrong that think-ing is. If your husband doesn't agree, suggest that the next time y'all are visiting his mama, he tell her how much weight she's gained and see what happens.

Another argument that a husband is likely to put forth, in order to continue this behavior without any interference, is that men are built differently from women and thus require constant scratching and/or rearranging. Now, without going into an anatomy lesson, I think we can all agree that things are complicated down there for both sexes. I also feel quite confident that, if we were to study the differences between men and women, side by side, we would come to the conclusion that both could conceivably feel the need to re-arrange and/or scratch themselves from time to time. May I point out, however, that unlike men, women have figured out a way to do both without the event becoming a national pastime.

Now, while I must concede that what men do in private is pretty much their own business (within limits, of course), who is to say what "private" really means? Certainly not a place where his wife—or anyone else—is present. Bottom line, husbands must be made to understand that some things (many things, in fact) simply do not take place around us. Scratching and rearranging, including "discreetly," here and there, are two of those things. Just like flatulence, which is dealt with extensively in another chapter, they can resolve each and every one of these urges by go-ing to the bathroom.

Ah, but if only it were that easy.

The Main Event

If you're one of these wives who has trouble convincing her hus-band that his habits are not only bizarre, but also a serious problem when it comes to keeping friends/relatives/jobs, you will need to take drastic measures. I address the problem of husbands and social situations in another chapter, with an entire methodology that is bound to cure what ails him. So you may want to review those suggestions and use the following as a last resort. On the other hand, if your husband is particularly embarrassing and refuses to yield to any motivation whatsoever, the following should be quite effective.

Go out and purchase a quality camcorder. If your husband complains, remind him about the happy memories you are creating, and how you must absolutely document them for posterity. Then e-mail his family and ask about their next reunion. Schedule your vacation, book tickets and a hotel room, then send out another e-mail, announcing that you and your husband will be attending. Copy your husband on the e-mail. When he tells you how much he appreciates your support, smile and bat your eyelashes. Then go out and buy a dozen blank tapes for the camcorder.

Your goal is to spend as much time as possible, during the next few months, filming your husband's activities. By "activities," of course, I do not mean simply soccer matches and backyard grilling, although you should definitely include those. I mean nose picking, mirror preening, sleep talking—anything and everything your husband does that needs to stop. Fortunately, much of his behavior, such as snoring and shower singing, will lend itself to the covert filming so necessary for good footage. Other acts, such as cover stealing, will require creative stealth. In some cases—the worst ones, no doubt—your husband could be so proud of himself that he might even be willing to perform for you. Either way, with the practice and perseverance so typical of Southern Girls, you can achieve your goal of creating a highly embarrassing video of your husband.

As you move toward the family reunion, be sure to build suspense for your audience. Tell them (and him) what a great home video you have and how excited you are to show it. Meanwhile, be sure to film your husband water-skiing, scoring a touchdown and achieving milestone victories in his life—like taking out the trash. That way, in addition to keeping him off your scent, you'll also have plenty of contrasting footage. Take care to edit accordingly.

On the night of the big movie, invite as many women as possible to watch the show. Grandmothers are good; old girlfriends are even better. If possible, show it on a night when your father-in-law and brothers-in-law are out. After all, you don't want anyone to congratulate him on his "masculine" behavior. Then show the video, and don't forget to narrate. "Oh, look! There's Bobby scoring a touchdown! And here, this is when he did the reading at church, on Christmas Day. Isn't he great? Now he's . . . oh, here he's picking his nose again. He does that."

Hopefully, after your family movie night, you won't have to worry about a thing. A few prolonged close-ups of your husband scratching his genitals should do wonders when it comes to spurring your mother-in-law into action. Worst-case scenario, you can always show the film as an "after-dinner movie," the next time your husband's boss visits. If his boss is a woman, you're set. But if his boss is a redneck, you may want to reconsider. After he sees your movie, he could give your husband a pat on the back and a huge raise.

In this case, the only thing you can do is invest that extra money in some good disguises for future public outings.

SEVEN

Cleaning and Chores: I Say a Little Prayer

I don't know about you, but I really hate cleaning bathrooms. Laundry, I can handle. Sweeping and vacuuming—no problem. Cleaning out the refrigerator? Okay. I'll even do the dishes and scrub the stove. But bathrooms? Yeeeech.

Now, like all good Southern Girls, I scrub for company, and I mean the baseboards (a place that would never occur to most men to even look). When relatives are coming, you could eat off my counters. It takes forever and usually lands me in the chiropractor's office, but at least I don't hear nasty comments from visiting relatives.

Well, actually, I do. My husband's stepmother once managed to make me feel awful about my clean house. She arrived from the airport, set down her suitcase, took one look and said, "Annabelle!

Your house is clean! I can't believe it!" then proceeded to laugh like I'd told her the best joke in the world.

Ah, family love. It just warms the heart, doesn't it?

Just because I clean, however, doesn't mean I enjoy it—especially when the cleaning involves a bathroom that has recently been used by a man. Now it's true, I am willing to concede, that unlike us, men must hit a target every time they pee. But first of all, that target is as big as the Mississippi. Second, they've been practicing since they were two—not just on commodes but on everything they could possibly think of. So you'd think that by the time men got to the ripe old age of thirty, they'd be hitting the bull's-eye every time. I mean, how hard can it possibly be? Alas, as every woman who has ever lived with a man knows, our toilet bowls runneth over. And just who do you think is going to be stuck cleaning those bowls? You, darlin'—pretty much like everything else you own.

Think of my aunt Nancy. Married to my mother's brother, she's put up with some serious Learned Helplessness during the past thirty years. After all, Charlie is a baby boomer, and boomers didn't have all the wonderful benefits of growing up as latchkey kids, like we did.[35]

Now there are lots of stories I could tell about my uncle, bless his heart, but I need a place to go for Thanksgiving, so I'll just pick one. Charlie and Nancy have a wonderful long-haired German shepherd named Max. One day Max, who weighs a whopping one hundred four pounds, got sick. As in, massive diarrhea. Doggie diarrhea.

---

[35]Case in point, my neighbor's eleven-year-old. That kid spends an inordinate amount of time alone, but every single week, he scrubs three bathrooms, vacuums and mops the floors and does the laundry. Assuming he doesn't become a serial killer, he's going to make some woman very happy one day.

Unfortunately, Max was sitting in the backseat of my uncle's brand-new pickup truck at the time, waiting for Charlie to return. When Charlie did return, he discovered his entire backseat—which was made of cloth, not leather—soaked with dog poop. As if this wasn't bad enough, poor Max had moved to the front so he wouldn't have to sit in his poop. So his rear end, which was covered in the mess, had stained the driver and passenger seats as well as the backseats.

Charlie covered his seat with a towel and his face with a bandanna and drove home, windows open. When he showed Nancy the truck, she was horrified, but suggested they clean it up as fast as possible, before the Carolina heat caked it on. She grabbed some towels, a bucket and cleaning supplies and headed for the door. Charlie stopped her.

"I can't do it," he said.

"Let's go," Nancy replied.

"I can't. I'll throw up."

"What? You think it's a day at the spa for me? Besides, you're the one who insisted on taking Max for a drive when he was acting funny."

"I'm sorry. I just can't do it," Charlie said. "I'm too grossed out."

Nancy paused. "I know you don't expect me to clean that up all by myself."

"I don't know. I don't care," Charlie answered. "Maybe we have to buy a new one."

"A new dog?"

"A new truck," he said. "I'm going downstairs." And then he did.

Learned Helplessness, in perhaps its finest moment ever. I'm tempted to crown my uncle with a gold medal in the Learned Helplessness Olympics, only I know there are probably even better stories out there, just waiting to be told. Charlie's definitely on the podium, though. Along with Mark and my daddy.

Another means by which husbands escape chores is procrastination, and most men are masters at it. This is probably because, when used upon an unsuspecting, unseasoned wife, it can be extremely effective. Many Southern Girls have said that whenever they come home from a trip, the hampers are overflowing with dirty clothes while all sorts of dishes, newspapers and trash remain scattered throughout the house. One Southern Girl, who was gone for two full weeks, returned and discovered that her husband hadn't run the dishwasher even once during her absence. Filthy plates, bowls, glasses and frying pans filled the kitchen.

"Oh," he said, when she asked why the place was such a mess, "I figured you'd take care of it."

This is the same husband who, when asked by his wife to do the laundry, begged off, saying, "Why can't you do it? All you have to do is put it in the machine and press a button."

Another Southern Girl managed to persuade her husband to share laundry responsibilities. Whenever it's his turn, however, he refuses to do it—even when he's out of underwear. For the longest time, she couldn't figure it out. Then she realized that he was wearing the same pair over and over.

Another husband has managed to ignore a leaky roof for months. "Doesn't it bother you," his wife said in what may be the biggest understatement of the year, "it's so damp when it rains?"

"If it bothers me, I don't look at it," he replied.

Still other husbands resort to more creative avoidance techniques. Going to the hardware store for "special equipment" before starting a task is especially popular. The added bonus for this strategy is that the husband can indulge in expensive gadgets while there. Yet woe to the wife who might even consider investing in some equipment for herself.

Rather than using the broom to sweep the floor—which would have taken just minutes—one husband spent hours going to and from Home Depot to purchase a special model. "It gets it up so much faster," he argued. He also insisted on buying two new vacuums to clean up plaster that had been left in their home—plaster that could have easily been swept up. With his new broom. Additionally, he has purchased a slew of cleaning products that are worth a small fortune, which form a collection under their sink. But how often does this husband actually sweep, vacuum or clean?

Take a guess.

Mark is a big fan of gadgets as well. He'll rarely begin a project without several trips to Home Depot. Once, he even bought a special[36] scrubbing machine. With its rotating pads, it was the perfect solution to cleaning the shower stall, he said—something that he was required to do, since I was pregnant at the time.

"If I buy this," he promised, "cleaning will be a breeze. You'll see."

Mark has had fun with his little machine. Since purchasing it six years ago, he's even used it. Twice.

(Everything I Do) I Do It for You

What's most amazing to me is that the husbands who accomplish the least around the house are often the ones who brag the most about what they've done—and a few things they haven't. After the birth of our second child, we hired a mother's helper. She made dinner and cleaned up the kitchen three nights a week. Several times, I overheard Mark talking on the phone, saying, "It's

---

[36]"Expensive."

great to come home and not have to make dinner or do the dishes," as if he had been slaving away at those chores for years.

Another Southern Girl recounted how her intense morning sickness[37] prevented her from even entering the kitchen, much less handling food. Not only did her husband have to cook, bless his little heart, but he also had to do the dishes during those three long and painful months of her first trimester. One night, with the kitchen a mess, he started storming around the house, complaining about how he did "everything." That was it, he bellowed. He couldn't take it any longer. He was sick and tired of doing the dishes, day after day, and he wouldn't do them any longer!

The wife's sister, who happened to be visiting—and who had made dinner that night—finally stood up. "What are you talking about?" she said. "I've done the past three loads of dishes!" The husband squared his shoulders and pointed at the skillets resting on the drying rack. "Well, I washed those pans," he retorted, to which the sister said, "No, sir! You did not. I did them myself last night."

We here at the Southern Girl's Institute are starting to wonder if maybe the husbands have been out back nipping at the old moonshine just a little too much.

The Grand Illusion

I remember the day I figured out that marriage would consist of more than cuddles, conversation and Cordon Bleu dinners. We were in premarital counseling at our local church, completing a detailed questionnaire about who would be responsible for the

---

[37] I hear you.

necessary household chores once we were married. We were to each fill one out then compare answers.

As I went down my list, it dawned on me that I'd never once considered who would vacuum, do the dishes or wash the clothes after I got married.[38] But how much of a problem could it be? Mark and I would agree on who did what, then abide by that.

My lackadaisical assumption was further confirmed when we shared our questionnaires. We were in such agreement, in fact, that I don't even remember what our various answers were—save two. Under "cooking," I had put my initials. Under "dishes," I had put his. Mark had put the same.

I heaved a sigh of relief and said, "I hate doing the dishes, but I love cooking." Mark replied, "Well, I hate cooking, but I don't mind the dishes."

It didn't take an *Apprentice* winner to realize that this was a golden opportunity. "If I never had to wash another dish as long as I lived," I said, "I'd be the happiest woman on the planet."

"And if I never had to cook another meal as long as I lived, I'd be the happiest man on the planet," Mark countered with a wide grin.

"Deal?"

"Deal." We shook.

And, oh, what a wonderful world it would be, if only things were that simple.

What a Fool Believes

For a few months, our arrangement worked well. Delighted to

---

[38]The fact that we had a full-time housekeeper when I was growing up may have contributed to this oversight.

play the new, adoring wife, I made Mark breakfast, lunch and dinner. I laid out cereal and milk, along with a bowl and spoon. I packed his lunch. I cooked elaborate dinners. In exchange, Mark cleaned up. In other words, he rinsed the dishes and put them into the dishwasher,[39] then washed the pots and pans and put them on the drying rack to dry. Now call me a Merry Maid, but when I "do the dishes," I make sure the table is cleared. I rinse the sink. I give the countertops a little squirt and clean them off. Ditto for the stove. And if I'm really feeling energetic, I'll sweep the floor. But apparently, I'm a real zealot, because not once were any of these things done when Mark "did the dishes." Along with putting away the pots and pans and running the disposal, these chores were left for the maid.[40] At least he didn't leave the dishes "soaking" in the sink, like so many husbands do.[41]

Prompted by full-time graduate studies, a part-time job and one very time-consuming internship, I soon wised up about meals and instituted the Twofer Rule, by which husbands are required to make their own breakfast and lunch in exchange for one deluxe gourmet dinner. Naturally, I told Mark that he should continue "doing the dishes" after that meal. And naturally, I did not tell him, I would come in afterward and finish.

"But you're not cooking my other meals?" he said, looking like he'd just spotted a tornado ripping through our living room. "We agreed that I wouldn't ever have to cook again." He emphasized the word "ever."

"You don't cook cereal. You pour it."

[39] We may have been dirt-poor grad students with carpet the color of cat poop, Harvest Gold appliances and a balcony that overlooked the Dumpster, but we had a dishwasher. I had my priorities straight.

[40] *Moi.*

[41] What I really like about that strategy is the way the grease coats all the glasses, as well as that red ring you get around the sink—especially when you've had spaghetti.

"You cook toast."

"No," I said, taking a deep breath, "you toast toast. And as long as breakfast and lunch do not consist of cooking—which they do not—I'm off the hook."

"But what if I want eggs for breakfast?" he said.

"No time. We're both racing to get to eight-o'clock classes."

"But I like eggs."

"You'll get high cholesterol," I said, turning away so he wouldn't see me laughing. "We can have eggs and French toast and stuff on weekends. But we can also go out for dinner."

"We can't afford to eat out every weekend."

"Okay, so I'll cook you eggs on weekends, as a bonus," I said. See? I'm reasonable. "But you'll clean. Per our agreement."

He paused, then said, "You know, what I really want is leftovers for breakfast. Like beef stroganoff, or that chicken thing you made last night. I like dinner for breakfast. I don't like breakfast food."

I closed my eyes. "We're graduate students, Mark. We can barely afford to pay tuition, much less eat meat three times a day. Besides, you'll get gout. Please just eat cereal and oatmeal like the rest of us—and don't tell me I have to boil the water for your instant oatmeal."

"I'm going to starve," he said with a whine, but he let it go. Then came his trump card, though. "Well, if you're not going to make breakfast, then I'm not going to put my cereal bowl in the dishwasher," he said.

Was a *Candid Camera* crew hiding behind our kitchen door? I looked at him. He was serious.

"Mark," I said, "I am not personally responsible for growing, harvesting, preparing, cooking and spoon-feeding every morsel that goes into your mouth. We had an agreement that I would cook and you would clean. I have done my part, including all the grocery shopping and most of the cleaning. And that has worked pretty well for the last six months. But you can doggone well put a bowl in the dishwasher, mister!"

You'd think that would have been the end of it, right? Oh, no. To this day, Mark still leaves his dishes in the sink—even when the dishwasher is empty and the sink is so clean it sparkles. Not only that, but within a year of that conversation, he began "forgetting" the dinner dishes as well, often waiting for days to do them. His excuse? He was "saving them."

Wise to the ways of Learned Helplessness, however, I decided to let the dishes stack up. To my surprise, it worked—although I did have to live with a perpetually disgusting kitchen (no small thing—can't say I recommend it). Every three days or so, Mark would cave in and start the task, while listening to a book on tape. Together with the dishwasher, the faucet and the clanking, it was enough to cause temporary deafness, but at least the dishes got done. Well, some of them. You see, the food had grown so hard by then that the pots rarely got clean. Also, since there were so many dirty dishes, only a few fit into the dishwasher, which meant that the sink stayed full. And, of course, the counters, sink and floors continue untouched.

Recently, the agreement became a moot point, anyway. Mark began working eighty-hour weeks at a new job, and he can't very well do the dishes at ten o'clock at night. So, in addition to cooking—and washing cereal bowls—I'm back to cleaning the kitchen as well. Thank goodness Mark does the accounting,[42] takes out the trash and throws clothes into the washer every now and then. After all, he is a Gen Xer, and if there's one thing Xers learned as kids, it's self-sufficiency. You can't come home every afternoon to an empty house, do all your chores and homework,

[42]A big job.

then make and eat dinner by yourself and not be at least somewhat self-sufficient, right? [43]

I Like to Move It

There is one household chore that Mark is really accomplished at, however. He calls it "cleaning up the house," and when it happens, it's very, very scary.

Now I like it when things are clean—very clean, in fact. I'm just not very good at cleaning. I'm also not very good at organizing, which, as strange as it may sound, can make me appear like a slob. I tend to create stacks—a leftover habit from my lawyer days. It is not without reason, therefore, that my husband calls my desk "the black hole." Eventually,[44] I get around to picking things up, but (a) that can take a while and (b) even when I do, I rarely know what to do with them.

All the magazines I'm keeping, for example, contain recipes that I want to clip. They're also full of brilliant ideas and engaging stories that I truly want to read. Of course, the fact that I can barely find time to take a shower each day—much less peruse four dozen magazines from cover to cover, with more arriving each month—somehow does not dissuade me from keeping these. And papers—they're all important. But who has time for filing? Especially since my files are woefully out-of-date. And clothes. I have too many, but it's expensive to throw them out. After all, what woman doesn't change sizes every few years? (And if you haven't, just wait until the baby years).

---

[43] And the boomers call us the "slackers."
[44] Don't you love the vagueness of this term?

> **Motto of the Ditcher Spouse:** "Use it or lose it."
> **Motto of the Hoarder Spouse:** "A place for nothing and nothing in its place."

Mark, on the other hand, is a compulsive ditcher. He loves to throw things out—as many things as possible, whenever possible, as fast as possible. I should have known, of course. After all, the man used to sleep on a mat with just one pillow, a sheet and a blanket. Next to that mat was a desk, a chair, a lamp and his computer. This was the entire contents of his room (which was basically his entire apartment) when I met him. He had obviously thrown out everything else he owned. But did I care? Of course not. I was too enthralled with his Tom Cruise looks and Nobel laureate mind to pay attention to any of these furiously flashing warning signals.

After we came home from the honeymoon and opened our wedding presents, Mark began his career of throwing things out. We were in Canada at the time, with plans to soon move back to the States, but for some reason, he decided to get rid of our china boxes. You know, those custom-made containers that fit plates, bowls and crystal and protect them from damage. Damage while moving. As in, from Canada back to the United States. And wouldn't it have been nice to have those boxes, to move those fragile dishes in? Apparently not, because Mark threw them all out—without telling me. I discovered it, as I often do, on the day of our move.

Possessed by some strange demon, Mark continued to throw things out over the years. In fact, if I didn't know better, I'd think he'd arranged some kind of kickback scheme with the local trash company. He threw out papers, books and magazines. He threw out clothes. He threw out dishes and silverware. He threw out spices that he deemed "useless"—and this, despite the fact that he couldn't distinguish between curry and coriander if his life depended on it. He threw out whatever he happened to stumble across that didn't strike him as "necessary," and trust me when I say that I had more than one hissy fit.

Now that we've been married almost twelve years, Mark has slowed down the ditching pace somewhat. To my amazement, he still throws things out occasionally, however—and it prompts just as many arguments. Just this weekend, he got rid of all the take-out menus that I had carefully collected during the past year and stacked next to our phone.

"I thought they were trash," he said casually.

"On the top shelf, inside the entertainment center?" I answered. "Didn't you notice the theme of that trash? As in, menus from local restaurants?"

He just shrugged. A few years ago, he went on a major holiday ditch, throwing out our decorations. He even threw away all of our Christmas-tree lights. This one really annoyed me, because he didn't tell me for two years—the day we were putting up the tree, in fact.

Just a few days ago, I made another shocking discovery. Mark had thrown away our dog. Yep. I naively believed that our precious little pup was on a shelf in the garage, waiting for that time when we would ceremoniously scatter his ashes. Mark and I had discussed his ash-scattering many times, in fact; we just hadn't found the right place. And we wanted it done right—or so I thought.

Suffice to say that when Mark admitted he had secretly thrown away the ashes, I was speechless. As if that's not bad enough, my thoughtful husband, who just happens to be a minister, also had the gall to throw those ashes in the trash can like a moldy piece of bread. Not over a scenic lake, across a nearby mountain, or on the floor of a peaceful forest. No, our faithful, favorite puppy—the one who broke both our hearts when he died at just eighteen months of age—was put to rest in a pile of garbage, out on the curb.

"I did bless the ashes first," Mark said, by way of explanation.

Not content to rob me of my precious valuables and loved ones, Mark also likes to reorganize them without telling me. He did the same thing to his stepmother, by the way—just stepped in one summer and reorganized her entire kitchen while she was gone. He even alphabetized her pantry. And to his utter amazement, she wasn't grateful.[45] After all, why couldn't she look for curry next to corn and Crisco? They each start with the letter C, right? Kind of like Mark's filing system, early on in our marriage, where he would file a hair dryer warranty under its brand name. Not "hair dryer." Not "hair." Not "appliance." No matter how much I pleaded, Mark insisted on filing it under "Braun"—and he just couldn't understand why I had trouble finding it.

Nowadays, instead of reorganizing my things, Mark throws them into boxes. I'm not sure which is worse, however—reorganizing or Box Hell. Picture an arm, moving across your desk and, in one fell swoop, removing everything in sight. We're talking papers, pens, office supplies, business cards, books and CDs. Once, he even dumped a coffee mug into the box, along with everything else.[46]

After "cleaning" my desk (which, strangely enough, doesn't actually involve cleaning or dusting), Mark then travels around the house, adding miscellaneous items to the box. I call it the Tasmanian Devil approach. Anything that doesn't belong to him and that is not neatly tucked away—whether on the floor or in the din-

[45]She was furious, in fact. Big surprise.
[46]At least it was empty.

ing room, living room, bathroom or kitchen—gets hurled into that box. Forget that the items might belong to the landlord, the neighbor, the dog. Into "my" box they go. Forget, too, that I might need them. Even urgently. Into the box they go.

Mark argues that all I have to do is take the box and—you guessed it—organize its contents. He further insists that if I don't do so within a few days, then I didn't really need those items to begin with. Oh, how wrong he is. Well, sort of.

First of all, there's the almighty "might." I might need those things someday. And for me, a hoarder, that's enough to make me keep them nearby. After all, who has time to sort through a stack of papers? Second, just because I don't go and get that missing piece of paper—it's a lot of effort to delve into a box of crap, I tell you[47]—doesn't mean I haven't already spent time working to replace it. Maybe I spent an extra hour on the Internet searching for the contact information on that missing business card. Maybe I made some phone calls. Maybe I even went and got another magazine. It won't stop me from hoarding, okay?

Now for you ditchers out there—and as much as it pains me to do this—here are some tips to get your spouse to cooperate with your organizational plans, without resorting to arbitration. First, don't touch that dial . . . er . . . stuff. Tell your husband that you would like to help him organize his things, then schedule a time for this. Do not be surprised if that time is woefully vague and/or several years into the future. The thought of anyone messing with their possessions is very scary for hoarders, so it may take a while to adjust to the idea.

When the scheduled day arrives, ask him how you can help, then follow his lead. Be patient, because he will have to go through every single item. No random (or secret) ditching. We hoarders

---

[47]Not that my stuff is crap. No, never.

appreciate your inspiration, which can be very clever at times, so feel free to make suggestions. But whatever you do, don't take over the process. This is not Burger King. You cannot have it your way.

The one good thing about Mark's box habit is that, despite the extra time and effort it costs me, once the place is "clean," I have room to accumulate more stuff. Also, thanks to his efforts, I do know I will survive without those items. This is a pretty big realization for a hoarder, and trust me when I say that it did not come without many years of soul-searching. And therapy—lots of therapy. Now I can safely say, with great confidence, that it's comforting to know that all my junk is in a box somewhere, in the garage, where I can find it. Most likely, it will stay in that box in my garage for the rest of eternity. But it doesn't mean I don't need it. So don't throw it out, Mark!

The moral of this story is that if you are a hoarder, beware and be afraid. Be very afraid. Find secret places to hide your stuff and don't tell anyone about them, especially your spouse. But if you're an organizer, remember that throwing things out and rearranging without permission is a surefire way to get your point across—your nasty little point. It will result in some arguments, and maybe even marriage counseling (which, I must warn you, can be quite expensive). But hey! What's a few thousand dollars and a little marital discord, compared to more closet space?

Surrender

Regardless of how much or little your husband helps around the house—and hopefully for you, he helps in different ways from my husband—there are ways to motivate him to do more. Much, much more.

First, remember that you are setting yourself up for disaster if you start doing everything yourself—something we seasoned wives advise you not to do, as vociferously as possible. Not only is this habit forming, but it also sends the message to your husband that there is an invisible house fairy who takes care of everything for men. Actually, there used to be an invisible fairy. Her name was "Mama," and she raised him. So forget Alice—it's Mama who doesn't live here anymore. Time to learn a little DIY, baby.

Let's take the laundry. Now, once your husband has learned how to actually use the washing machine and dryer, you may—and should—revert to sharing the laundry. But until then, Southern persistence must prevail. Forget the socks—the ones he's been forgetting—until he finds himself sockless on the day of his big interview.

If he is particularly stubborn in this area, and either allows the dirty clothes to stack up on the floor or—as the husband of a certain editor likes to do—simply replaces them with more dirty clothes, in the same spot, drastic measures must be taken. You basically have two options. The first is to go ahead and pick up his dirty socks and underwear every morning, but fold them and return them to his drawer, next to the clean socks and underwear.

Obviously, you will need to be very regular about this so his drawer is kept full. You will also need to be patient. When he finally realizes something is amiss,[48] just be honest. "Dirty? I don't know. I just pick up your socks and put them back in your drawer every morning. The stuff in the dirty clothes hamper? Now that, I wash."

Your second option is to make picking up his clothes a daily chore, and place it under the motivational system described below.

[48]Try and stem your revulsion. This could take several months.

But personally I think he'll get the message with the first strategy, which will hopefully lead him straight to the old W & D. Show him how to use them, and be sure to write out instructions and post them above the machines. Not that he'll remember they are there—or find them or even be able to read your handwriting. But at least you can insist he look at them when he starts asking you what button to push.

The second principle to keep in mind when selecting chores for your husband is that it helps greatly if you can make a man feel special—heroic, even—by helping you out. When I lived with my roommate Anita, before marrying Mark, our bathtub would often become clogged with long blond hair. Mixed with soap and shampoo, it was so disgusting that we both gagged every time we had to pull it out of the drain. Fortunately, I was dating Mark, who didn't mind lending a hand. Literally. Although he would roll his eyes, he would whip that mess out of there, throw it in the trash and strut into our living room like he'd just eliminated the *Exxon Valdez* oil spill. Moral of the story: men need to feel special, even when cleaning out the drain. Be sure to thank 'em, too. Gratitude goes a long way.[49]

Third, be advised that men like to do things their way. Wait— I probably didn't say that clearly enough. Let me try that again. Ahem. MEN LIKE TO DO THINGS THEIR WAY. And unless you are his mother, his father, his sibling, his boss, his friend, his neighbor or basically anyone he either knows, buys coffee from or happens to spot while walking across the street, he will not take your advice. A scientific study from the Southern Girl's Institute concluded that a man is 387 percent more likely to listen to a homeless begger, the trashman or a stranger he has chatted with, however briefly, than his wife. The good news, however, is that if

---

[49]Don't write a thank-you note, though. That's taking things just a little too far.

you've been very good to your trashman at Christmas each year, or generous with the panhandlers, they just might be willing to offer your husband a few tips on your behalf.

There Are Some Things Money Can't Buy. . . .

New sheets: $85
New underwear: $100
New silk shirt: $180
New towels: $250
New washing machine: $450
Husband learning to do laundry all by himself: priceless

Once you've finally convinced your husband to help out, even just a little, let him carry it through to the end, no matter how catastrophic the results may be—and trust me when I say that there will be disasters. He will shrink your sweater and ruin your favorite silk shirt. He will dye your white underwear pink and spill bleach on your designer towels. But believe me, the cost of replacing these items will pale in comparison to the joy you will feel the day you see your husband mastering those complicated machines.

I've learned the hard way that as long as men are doing what they need to be doing, it's just not worth it to complain. One Southern Boy I know insists on ironing one shirt every night before going to bed.[50] No matter how much his wife argues about the time he could save, if only he would iron two or three, he insists

---

[50]Now this boy's mother deserves an award.

on his little routine. But this Southern Girl is one wise woman. "I've stopped suggesting," she said. Preach it, sister.

The same thing goes for the bathroom and the kitchen, and any other area where he might deign to pitch in. One Southern Girl called home early in the evening to say that she'd be late. She told her husband that if he could wait just a bit, she'd make Mexican soup, one of his favorite dishes. Since he'd been home all day, he offered to make it. She walked him through the recipe over the phone while driving.

"It's supereasy," she said. "You take one can of corn, one can of tomatoes with chilis, one can of pinto beans, one can of cheese soup and one can of tomato soup and put them all into a pot on the stove to heat." Once he had located and opened all the cans, she continued. "Now take some celery and onions and chop them up. Put them in a bowl with a can of chicken broth and nuke them until they're soft. Then add that to the soup."

She hung up and continued driving while her husband proceeded with the recipe.[51] When he called back, she gave him one final instruction. "Take the tortillas and chop them up. Then grab the shredded cheese and leftover rice from the fridge. Put everything on the table and let the kids add whatever they like to the soup."

"Okay," said the husband. "I'm almost done. See you in a bit."

When the wife got home, no one had eaten the soup and the kids were starving. "What's the matter?" she said. Then she spotted the soup. Instead of the creamy version she was used to, it was light and clear—and full of water.

"What did you do to it?" she asked.

"Nothing!" he insisted. "I made it exactly the way you said."

---

[51]This was in Atlanta, where it takes at least forty minutes to drive across the street.

"Then why is it so watery?"

"Because it's soup," he answered.

Confused, she just stared.

"You make soup with water," he insisted. "So I started off with a pot of water."

"Did I tell you to start off with a pot of water?" she said.

"No," he admitted in the tone of a five-star chef speaking to a wayward underling. "But I figured you forgot. Because that's how you make soup. With water. And, by the way, it tastes just fine."

Of course, like the wise Southern Girl that she is, she just nodded. Then she served him that delicious homemade soup for his next three dinners.

Mmm, mmm, good!

Don't You Want Me

Finally, no matter how much your husband is willing to help around the house, you will still want to implement a motivational system. This, by the way, is where things will really come together, in terms of long-term chore training. But first, a story.

For years after we got married, I tried to convince Mark to get a dog. I bargained. I reasoned. I begged. Finally, when I was out of town one week, a neighbor dropped by with some puppies. The next thing I knew, Mark was greeting me at the airport with an adorable eight-week-old mutt. It was a miracle! The best gift he's ever given me. We named him after a Confederate hero, Colonel John Mosby, of the famed Mosby's Rangers. And yes, in case you're wondering, this is the same dog whose final place of repose is now a landfill somewhere in DeKalb County, Georgia.

I had never trained a dog, so I set about reading up on the subject. I learned that the most important thing is to keep the puppy in a crate when no one is around and at night when he's sleeping. This will make him feel warm and safe, while also preventing him from soiling the floor, because dogs won't wet where they sleep.[52] Second, the owner must take the puppy outside at very specific times (after meals, after playing with him, before bedding down for the night), and always to the same spot. This creates a routine, which is all important for the training to work.

Once outside, and as soon as the dog begins his business, the owner should utter a catchphrase several times in order to create a trigger. For example, I used to say, "Hurry up!" The idea is that, after the dog has wet seventy or eighty times while hearing that phrase, he'll go automatically (which is particularly helpful during storms, car trips and hurricanes). Finally, as soon as he has taken care of business, the owner must reward him with lots of affirmation. She should be very enthusiastic so that the dog gets the message that going to the bathroom is one huge party. Yay!

The key to all this—and the one where most people fail—is to withhold affirmation until the puppy has done his job. Even though he may be the most adorable thing you've ever seen, and certainly worthy of your undying attention and affection, you mustn't cuddle or play with him at will. You do that after he has peed or pooped. And only after he has peed or pooped.

Unfortunately, even though it's the most compassionate and quickest way of training a dog, a lot of people refuse to carry through with this plan. Some think that crates are cruel, when they actually feel like comfy little dens to the dog. But most can't resist the temptation to play with the animal, rather than saving that for positive reinforcement. What people don't realize, however, is that their affection must only be restricted for a short time.

---

[52]Be sure the crate has a comfy duvet or pillow and isn't too big; otherwise the puppy will wet on one side and sleep on the other.

Once the dog is trained—which should take no more than a few months—they can freely hug, kiss and snuggle him for the rest of his life.

These same people, interestingly enough, are often the ones who believe that rubbing a dog's nose in it or yelling at him is going to teach him a lesson—actions that are completely ineffective, if not downright abusive. The reason is that while it may seem as if the little dog is contrite, he's merely cowering in the face of his owner's anger. Just minutes, if not seconds, after a puppy has wet, he has forgotten completely about it. So when the little thing gets yelled at, spanked or pushed into his mess, he has no clue what's happening. All he knows is that his owner is furious, and for the life of him, he can't figure out why. As a result, the dog becomes anxious and can't obey, no matter how hard he tries, which is a big reason that dog pounds are bursting at the seams.

Now I would be totally remiss to suggest that men are like dogs. Nooooo. Men are human beings with brilliant brains, warm hearts, strong bodies and the ability to think, reason and use power drills. So it would be grossly unfair to compare them to their canine companions. However, if there's anything married women know, it's that men are just a little bit like dogs. They want to do the right thing, but they aren't quite sure how, where and when to do it. They don't respond to yelling or punishment, but do incredibly well with positive affirmation. They also long for affection, but they need training to win that. Lots of training. And until they get that training, they'll make a huge mess all over the house.

In order to train your husband to really do chores, and do them well, you will need to set up a chore chart. Remember that piece of paper your mother tacked onto the refrigerator with a magnet when you were a little kid? The one where she kept track of the tasks you were supposed to do each day—things like making the bed, cleaning your room, setting the table and doing your homework? The same principle applies here.

Take a piece of paper and draw a graph with vertical and horizontal rows. Then, with your husband, determine who will be responsible for the daily and weekly chores around the house. If he balks, just skip ahead and explain the reward system described below. Next list the chores that he will be doing (I use the term loosely) on the left side of the chart. At the top, list the days that the chores are to be done.

For example, if your husband has agreed to make the bed and do the dishes after dinner each day, they should be listed on the left side of the chart. Don't forget the obvious ones—which aren't really chores, but feel like it to men—like hanging up his jacket, putting his cereal bowl in the dishwasher and, in some cases, even flushing the toilet. For other items, like taking out the trash, you may want to pick two or three days a week when he should do that, regardless of how full the bin may be. You don't want to burden him with any executive decisions. Otherwise, well, it will be you who's taking out the trash, and that defeats our purpose.

The top of the chart should show the days of the week. The left side of the chart should show the chores. Don't forget to distinguish between summer ones (like cutting the grass) and winter ones (like snow blowing). List everything you can think of, then black out the days of the week when the various tasks need not be done.

You will then need to purchase two packages of stickers. One kind will be used for a task well done; the other, for a task that was not done—or done poorly. My grandmother used to use black hearts and gold stars for my mother, but I think that's just a little morbid, don't you? Especially for a toddler.[53] I'd go with a theme of his choice, whether sports- or cartoon-related. Anything to

[53]Actually, this may explain a lot.

inspire the guy. But trust me, his real motivation will be in the rewards.

This is the fun part. Because, after working hard all week, your husband gets to play—with you! For daily chores, you'll probably want a plain vanilla reward. You know, just your average romp in the hay. You and your husband, doing what you're supposed to be doing on a Saturday morning. Or Saturday night. Or, hey, even Sunday morning, before church. You're married, right? And this is what married couples do—especially when the wife doesn't have to worry about vacuuming. Hint, hint.

For the weekly chores, you can choose something a little more interesting—whatever floats his boat (and yours). You know, that little special something that you don't usually have time for on other occasions. And finally, for the toughest chores, he should get something truly extraordinary. I'll leave the details up to you. Just be sure you're comfortable with it, then close the curtains.

Also, you may want to create a little chore chart for yourself. After all, we need to be motivated to do housework, too, right? If you want the same rewards as your husband, go for it. He'll probably even help with your tasks so everything gets done faster. Other options for your rewards might include date nights at the local theater, mandatory viewing of romantic comedies and visits to your mother. The possibilities are endless.

The trick with any reward system, but especially your husband's, is to be creative and very, very specific. Graphic, even. Remember, you're married. It's okay to have sex, even lots of it. And you want your husband thinking about all of those rewards throughout the week so he'll work very hard to get them. Just make sure to use a reward "code" if you're posting the chart on the fridge. After all, you never know when the preacher might come to visit.

Finally, be certain that your husband accomplishes all his tasks before leaping into bed. Check the corners. Look under the sofa. Open the dishwasher. Correct where necessary. Entice as needed. And no matter what, always follow through with your promises. World peace depends on it.

EIGHT

Spending Time Together: Can't Get Enough of Your Love, Babe

Oh, the joy of spending time together! The very goal of marriage, after all, is to spend every possible moment with your beloved, wrapped in his arms, sharing the most intimate details of your hearts. Dating was wonderful, when it comes to spending time together, but marriage will be a thousand times better.

Hmmm. Here's the problem. When you're dating, being together is as easy and fulfilling as an afternoon on the beach. You go out, you have fun, you come home—end of story. But for married couples, spending time—quality time—together can be as tough as a pair of never-pedicured feet.

First and foremost is actually finding that time to spend together—something that used to be like breathing. Once you're married, work responsibilities, social events and family commitments tend to crowd out those wonderful old date nights. Remember the art shows, restaurant openings and theme parties? They're not over, by any stretch. (At least until you have kids, anyway.) But they will have a tendency to creep toward predictability—and get crowded out by a regular routine of work, gym, dinner, TV and bed.

Marriage, quite simply, tends to make us much more functional. Take going to the movies. When a couple is dating, this is a leisurely activity. They park the car together, stroll over to the ticket window together and stand in line together. Still holding hands, they wait in yet another line for popcorn and Cokes, then search for their seats together. It doesn't matter if they miss the first ten minutes of the film, or if they have to sit in the front row and crane their necks for the next two hours. Just as long as they're together!

After the wedding, going to the movies is more like a Marine combat exercise. After synchronizing their watches, a husband and wife will move out. He parks the car. She goes after the tickets. He races inside, observes the popcorn lines, slips into the shortest one. Meanwhile, she's signaling from the perimeter. They make cell-phone contact; she heads inside to scope out the terrain. Phase one complete, the husband enters the theater. A few hand signals later, and they've located each other. He hurls himself across the gauntlet. Finally, with mere seconds to spare, he captures the seat. Mission accomplished!

Then there's the fatigue factor inherent to marriage. Courtship and weddings require a huge emotional investment. You've been channeling a lot of energy into getting to know each other, from evenings and weekends on the town to pondering the engagement and finally planning your big day. Then you had the wedding, which leaves most people feeling like a six-year-old the morning after a sugar binge. Mark and I were so exhausted after our ceremony we could barely even remember it.[54] As a result, we hung the DO NOT DISTURB sign on our honeymoon door so much the maids had to think we were sex maniacs[55] when we were actually just sleeping.

Dating and weddings are also expensive. Restaurant dinners, movies, shows, drinks—it all adds up. And unless your daddy happens to be privy to Coca-Cola's secret recipe, you've probably just tapped into some hefty wedding capital. That means debt—and we haven't even begun to talk about student loans. So if you're like most newlyweds, you may not have a lot of extra cash on hand for socializing right now.

Finally—and this is one of life's greatest ironies—the big incentive for romance is pretty much out the window now that you're married. That doesn't mean romance is completely over and done with, only that your husband won't be quite as motivated. You used to be the prey, you see. Date nights were the hunt. But now the hunt is over, and the prey is waiting at home, in bed, wearing a negligee. Suffice to say that his enthusiasm for spending a hundred bucks and two hours at a restaurant is a thing of the past. Especially since the prey has already fed the hunter dinner, anyway.

Talk Talk

In order to learn how to spend quality time with you, new husbands must first come to understand the definition of "conversation."

---

[54]Thanks to the photos, I do know for sure that I married him, however—just in case anybody is wondering.

[55]I won't go there.

Women are experts at this fine art, having prolifically engaged in it since infancy, and no doubt before. But most men—a few chatterboxes notwithstanding—find it a very complicated concept. Not only that, but what was merely confusing grows even more muddied by the waters of "male-speak," as men grow older.

Male-speak takes place when two or more men engage in a shared activity—playing sports, fixing things, grilling steaks— while making comments to, about and in spite of one another. To the uninitiated, these comments may appear to be conversation. They are not. They are merely random statements that may or may not be logically connected, and that may or may not be made in response to a question or other statement. Male-speak, simply put, is talking.

Conversation, on the other hand, revolves around a little-known activity called "listening." Unlike male-speak, or talking, conversation consists of comments that are logically connected to one another, typically made in response to a statement or question, after the speaker has "listened" to the other speaker. Listening is a very important activity, and without it, conversation cannot take place. Sadly, however, it is fast becoming extinct among both sexes. It is so rare among the male population, however, that anthropologists are now questioning whether men are still capable of listening. What they are capable of, we know, is pretending to listen.

A Sample Conversation over Drinks

Suzanne: "Hey, Joanne. You look terrible."
Joanne: "I'm okay."
Suzanne: "Just okay?"
Joanne: "Well, yeah."
Suzanne: "What's going on?"

Joanne: "Oh, my job search. It's so depressing. Sir? Can you bring me a cosmopolitan, please?"

Suzanne: "Make that two. Whoa, check out that waiter!"

Joanne: "No kidding. Probably married, though."

Suzanne: "Or gay. Is there anything I can do to help with the job search, honey?"

Joanne: "You're sweet. I feel like I've tried everything. The market is so slow."

Suzanne: "You know, I just got a promotion."

Joanne: "You're kidding me! Congratulations! You totally deserve it."

Suzanne: "Thanks. But what I'm saying is that I may be able to help you."

Joanne: "Really?"

Suzanne: "E-mail me your résumé tomorrow. I can't promise, but I'll see what I can do."

Joanne: "You're amazing! Thank you."

Suzanne: "Hey, what are friends for?"

A Sample Male-Speak over Drinks

Steve: "Hey, Joe. What's shaking?"

Joe: "Oh, you know, still looking for a job. Whoa, check out that Ferrari!"

Steve: "Cool. Let's order some appetizers. But don't get that cheese thing. It made me sick last week. Hey, did I tell you I got promoted?"

Joe: "Sounds good. Waitress! Could you bring us two beers and . . . let's see . . . maybe some wings? No, how about one of those cheese things? We had it last week and it was really good."

Steve: "So how's the job search?"

Joe: "No leads at all. The market is dead. Any openings at your company?"

Steve: "Great. Yeah. I just got a promotion."

Joe: "Umm, this cheese thing is good. You should try it."

Steve: "No, thanks. So what kind of interviews have you been doing?"

Joe: "Well . . . I ran into Dave last week. He works for BellSouth."

Steve: "Dave from high school? Does he still do that snorting thing with his nose?"

Joe: "Yeah, same as before. Hilarious! So what were you saying about your company?"

Steve: "Whoa, hot waitress, huh?"

Joe: "No kidding. Ah, just in time—the beers. To friends!"

Steve: "Yeah! Friends! Hey, get a load of that Ferrari!"

Young wives may find it hard to believe that their husbands do not exist in order to hang on their every word. After all, these men have just spent months, if not years, doing just that—long, extended conversations during which they appeared to be listening to every sound their girlfriends uttered. Unfortunately, the key word here is "appeared."

"Men never listen," confirmed my uncle Charlie, a thirty-year veteran of the marriage trenches. "We just pretend to. We nod and say 'Un-huh, un-huh' and occasionally ask a question or two, but we're not listening. Hardly ever, anyway—and even then only long enough to get the gist of what somebody's saying."

"But why?" I said, trying but failing to keep the dismay from my voice. After all, it's one thing to suspect the truth, another to hear it put so bluntly.

"Too much on our minds," Charlie said. "We're thinking

about work or some problem. And we're always trying to get as much done as possible. Listening feels like a waste of time."

"But women are busy, too! Busier than men, for that matter."

Charlie took a sip of his beer and laughed. "I'm just telling you the way it is."

"I find this hard to believe."

"It's a guy secret."

I shook my head. "And you think all men do this?"

"I know they do. Not listening is natural," Charlie said. "If we do listen, it takes major rewiring."

"Doesn't Nancy get mad?" I pressed. "I always know when Mark isn't listening, and it makes me really angry."

Charlie laughed again. "Nah, you don't know."

"Come on!"

"We're really good at faking it," he said. "We may get busted every now and then, but the longer we're married, the better we get. I'm telling you. You don't know even half the times Mark isn't listening."

I took this assessment to my father, one of the best defense attorneys in the state of North Carolina.[56] Surely, for his work, he had learned how to listen extremely well?

"Not really," he admitted.

"But if you know it makes us mad, why don't you listen?" I asked.

"You women talk too much!" he said with an impish grin. "How could we listen to everything you say?"

He does have a point. Linguistic experts report that the average man uses between two thousand and ten thousand words per day. By contrast, the average woman uses between seven thousand and twenty-five thousand words each day. Some will say that this

---

[56]No bias here.

means women talk more than men. And no doubt, this is true. Women talk, love to talk, and talk a lot, whereas men have a natural tendency toward—shall we say—silence. But I'm also convinced that these statistics are misleading. After all, what woman does not need to repeat herself at least three times whenever she says something to her husband? I figure that accounts for at least a few thousand words a day, if not more.

So listening—the lost art. How to revive it? Well, frankly my dear, ya got me. I have been trying for twelve long years and have yet to see much success. Sorry. In the meantime, however, the best thing we can realistically hope for is conversation that revolves around interesting topics. That way, if your husband isn't listening, at least you'll enjoy what you're talking about. But this, too, is a training ground, and you'll need to start small.

Choose a familiar arena—say, sports. Then explain the way it works. For example, acceptable conversation, you must tell your husband, does not consist of recapping the pitching stats of Greg Maddux (star pitcher for the Atlanta Braves). On the other hand, discussing the divorce of Chipper Jones (star hitter for the Braves) after he impregnated a Hooters waitress and embarrassed his darling wife—who just happened to be on the cover of a local magazine the very same month this awful thing happened, bless her heart—definitely does. Ditto for talking about John Rocker (former Braves pitcher), who embarrassed all seven million people in the great state of Georgia after talking to a *Sports Illustrated* reporter and acting like a dumb, racist redneck.[57]

And they say women don't like sports!

---

[57] Wait—that's redundant.

Acceptable Conversation Topics	Unacceptable Conversation Topics
• Current marital status of Angelina Jolie	• Current measurements of Angelina Jolie
• Current hairstyle of Oprah	• Your current hairstyle
• Pecs of any sports player	• Stats of any sports player
• Your best friend's wedding	• Your best friend's divorce
• Princess Diana conspiracy theories	• Computer piracy theories
• How to clean out the litter box	• How to fix the mailbox

Quality Time

In addition to finding the time to be together, newlyweds may also struggle over what it means to actually be "together," believe it or not. During our newlywed years, going to a party with 250 people qualified as a "date night" for Mark, even if he spent the entire evening on the other side of the room. Which he did do. More than once. We're talking, not even a wave from the male huddle. Not that I'm bitter or anything, mind you.

"But we're out together having fun," he would say when I protested. "That is a date night."

"No, date nights are when we're alone—just the two of us," I'd answer.

"But aren't you having a good time? So what's the problem?"

The problem, of course, is that when women say "together," we mean "alone." As in, cue the slow dance music. When men say "together," they mean "within shouting distance"—which can actually becoming a self-fulfilling prophecy, if they're not careful. So it might be helpful to explain to your new husband that there are three different ways of spending time together—quality time, that is.

The first is alone time, also called a "date night." The second is "couple time," and the third is "group time." There does exist a fourth kind of quality time, which is called "family time" and involves spending time with family members of either spouse. Please note, however, that family time is not usually considered quality time. Not only that, but the more prolonged family time is, the more date nights will be required to offset any emotional damage inflicted during family time.[58]

Also, lengthy car trips do not qualify as date nights, even if you are alone. They are a means to an end, not the end in itself. Depending on the situation, including the destination, the amount of time spent in the car and the time of the month, they could become an end, however. Consider yourself warned.

Now recognizing how confusing these terms can be for new husbands, we asked our in-house attorney here at the Southern Girl's Institute[59] to define the various concepts from a legal perspective.

Conjugal Quality Time

Date Night (dāt nīt): A period of time generally lasting between two and four hours during which a husband and

---

[58]Some of those date nights might even need to take place in the counselor's office.
[59]Yours truly.

wife exchange meaningful conversation in a setting outside their home without the presence, interference or participation of friends, neighbors, colleagues, family members or anyone else who might impede the verbal intimacy mandatory for said date night. Please note that brief and casual conversations with bartenders, waiters and strangers do not deter or detract from the aforementioned intimacy. Accepting or making cell phone calls of any kind, checking e-mail and surfing the Internet, however, as well as getting drunk and acting like a moron do. In this case, said date night is immediately rendered null and void.

Couple Time (kŭp' əl tīm): A period of time generally lasting between two and four hours during which a husband and wife interact (talk, converse, chatter, chat, speak) with one, two or three other couples, preferably those who are married or in a long-term, committed and/or monogamous relationship, while also usually enjoying food and/or an activity (movie, game, show, game show) together. Interaction with other couples during said couple time does not preclude husband from meaningful conversation, however sporadic, with wife, in a manner to be determined by wife in accordance with wife's interest in engaging in meaningful conversation with other women during said couple time. Please note that should husband spend too much time talking with other husbands during couple time, conflict may result. Should husband spend too much time talking to other wives during couple time, conflict will result. In this case, said couple time is immediately rendered null and void.

Group Time (grōōp tīm): A period of time generally lasting between two and four hours, typically scheduled around a specific activity (movie, game, show, game show) during which a husband and wife interact (talk, converse, chatter, chat, speak) with seven or more people who have gathered for the sole purpose of interacting together. Please note that all rules governing Couple Time apply equally to Group Time, in particular the requirement for meaningful interaction with wife to the exclusion of any men, women, husbands, wives, children or pets who may be present and desirous of attention, and in complete accordance with wife's interest and instructions, whether verbal, silent, conscious or unconscious.

Date nights, in particular, are very important to understand. The reason for this, which will be of significant interest to your spouse, is that when date nights are carried out correctly—meaning, when they involve significant, sustained interaction between husband and wife—they will impart a great sense of well-being to the wife. It is this sense of well-being, appropriately and adequately bestowed upon the wife, that creates warm and loving feelings for the wife. And warm and loving feelings smooth the way, like shots in a singles bar, toward sex. It's a one-way street, gentlemen, and there are no detours. So put down the newspaper and tune in.

Your husband reading the sports pages, for example, while you fume is not "quality time"—even though you may be alone together. Ditto for the two of you checking e-mail on separate computers in the same room. Him cutting the grass while you sit on the front porch with a margarita is better, but still not what we're aiming for. The two of you visiting the Margaret Mitchell House, attending the ballet or shopping, on the other hand, is. Provided, of course, that the shopping does not take place in a pawnshop, gun shop, sports shop, military clothing shop or used-car lot.

Going to a professional ball game can also qualify as a date night, provided that (a) you love that sport and (b) you're not sitting next to people you know—in which case it becomes either couple time, group time or the dreaded "family time," depending on who they are. Likewise, when dining out, eating at a restaurant where the entrées do not exceed five dollars and come with a choice of fries or onion rings is not an acceptable date night, whereas any place that serves steak (the obvious exception being the local all-you-can-eat buffet) probably is.

Don't assume, however, that spending a lot of money is the key to a successful date night. We don't mind it, and we certainly won't take out a restraining order if you want to, but it's not required. In other words, cheap date nights are absolutely allowed. What we're looking for is good intentions, a little creativity and a lot of romance. And romance, contrary to public perception, doesn't always come with a cost. For example, a picnic on a grassy knoll with bread, cheese and wine qualifies as a wonderful date night (even during the day). Unless it's raining, of course. But should that happen, just turn the situation to your advantage and take a walk in the rain, thereby creating another highly successful—and inexpensive—date night. Or how about a visit to the local museum? Or a scenic drive? It's all about the motives, boys. Not the money.

Now, ladies, I need to add a little caveat, here. First of all, you must be very patient with your mate. It will take time for him to learn the difference between acceptable and unacceptable date nights—and some of this is your fault. After all, when it comes to spending time together, your entire courtship could be construed as a huge bait-and-switch exercise, from his perspective. Think about it. Until your wedding, you were willing to do just about anything to spend time with your beloved. Baseball games? "Sure, I'd love to, honey!" NASCAR championship? "I can't wait!" And "Oh, I'd just love to help you look for those golf balls in that snake-filled swamp, darlin'!"

Once you're married, however, this pretty much changes overnight. Spend a Saturday in a 100-degree baseball stadium? "I don't think so." "I'm sorry—you want us to wash what today? Your car? Sweetie, do you know what that will do to my nails?" Hunting? "No, no, no. I can't stand the thought." "Well, I know I did, but I just didn't want to hurt your feelings." "No, I don't like venison, actually. I used to spit it out when you weren't looking."

So be gentle on the boys, ladies. They are very, very confused right now.

Acceptable Date Nights	*Unacceptable Date Nights*
• Shopping	• Hunting
• Picnic in the park	• Football in the park
• Taking a scenic drive	• Repairing a hard drive
• Touring the Margaret Mitchell House	• Painting the doghouse
• Dining out	• Passing out
• Movie and dessert	• DVD and a snack
• Author lecture	• Mother-in-law lecture
• Evening at the theater/ballet/opera/museum (provided no nudity is involved)	• Evening at the ballpark/football field/basketball court (unless nudity is involved)

Couples who qualify as couples, for the sake of couple time, are any couples you enjoy spending time with. In other words, two of your husband's old roommates do not qualify as a "couple"— unless they're gay, in which case you might want to ask yourself why your husband was living with them, alone in an apartment, in the first place. In the same vein, neither do work colleagues, even if married, qualify as a couple—unless they are very good friends. And need I mention that an evening with someone's boss and spouse is not quality couple time? That's work, honey.

The same goes for group time. Basically, you must both enjoy the company you're with, and enjoy interacting with them, while engaging in a fun activity of some sort—even if that activity is just eating. In other words, cheering along, week after week, with the people sitting next to your season seats at Panthers games does not qualify as group time. Going to a surprise birthday party that has been thoughtfully arranged by your husband to include all of your friends, however, does.

Vacation

In a category all by itself are vacations—the ultimate quality time. But before you get all misty-eyed, you'd better compare notes. I know a young couple who has elected to spend their honeymoon at an amusement park. All they want to do is ride the rides for days on end. As with many nineteen-year-olds,[60] going to an amusement park is how they enjoy spending time together, and I think it's great.

However, if my husband were to take me to an amusement park for our honeymoon, the honeymoon would be over.

---

[60]Yes, they're nineteen and getting married. I know.

Generally speaking, my idea of a vacation includes sand, waves and regular appearances of waiters bearing frosty drinks. Skiing is also good, under the right circumstances—meaning, a few midday hours on the slopes, lunch on the deck, followed by après-ski, a roaring fire and perhaps a nice glass of port. Don't forget the Jacuzzi.

The poor man's version of this counts, too, of course: a trip to the mountains in a cute log cabin. Provided I am not required to go on hikes, that is. I'll wait by the fire while y'all check out the view way on up there, thank you very much. And finally, if we should win the lottery—or maybe just get a decent tax refund—I'd be thrilled with a little European jaunt, especially where afternoon tea, shopping and prolonged dinners are involved.

Now Mark, on the other hand, enjoys active vacations. He likes to hike, play golf and tennis and go places. Even when we were in Hawaii for our honeymoon, he insisted on seeking out every historical landmark within a hundred miles. I'll never forget the time we went hunting for some old fort on the island of Maui. We drove all over that dang place before parking and searching for it on foot. Finally, as we wiped the sweat from our brows and took a rest from all the trekking, we realized that we were standing on the "fort." It was a heap of old rocks.[61]

Mark also loves museums—especially ones that relate to military history. Battlefields are a big draw, too. Like many Southern men, Mark's goal is to visit every single Civil War battlefield before he dies.[62] And I say, go for it, honey. I'll be at home holding down our fort.

---

[61]This is one of those moments where it's very difficult not to say, "I told you we should have stayed at the pool."

[62]Officially, Mark's a Yankee, but he went to Washington & Lee University, which gives him Southern credentials—and Southern tendencies. Thank goodness.

Acceptable Vacations	Unacceptable Vacations
• A trip to Hollywood	• A trip to Dollywood
• Time in the mountains	• Time in the woods
• Anywhere on the beach	• Anywhere that leaks
• Skiing	• Golfing
• A cozy log cabin	• A leaky tent

Needless to say, vacations have been a big area of compromise for us. Typically, we agree to spend one day on the beach followed by a day filled with activities, which makes us both happy. Then again, nowadays, Mark is so exhausted from his job that my vision of the ideal vacation—lolling around, doing nothing—tends to be much more appealing than it used to be. Sometimes, it just takes a little patience. (Even if it was twelve years' worth.)

Of course, your husband may have very creative ideas about how to vacation. I was surprised at how many Southern Girls said that their husbands wanted them to take a camping vacation. And not in a $250,000 recreational vehicle, either. We're talking a tent—with no electricity or running water. Now I don't know about you, but does it really take a boy wonder to figure out that this is a bad idea? Heck, it's not like we're going to feel particularly romantic in a vinyl sleeping bag after eating hobo stew and marshmallows, now, are we? And forget those stupid car commercials—the ones where adorable girls are hiking and camping all over the place. They're trying to sell cars to men, okay? Just like their boobs—they're not real, boys!

I was also shocked to hear how many husbands thought that hunting and fishing would be fun for us. So okay, gentlemen, let's get something straight: killing—even something we like to eat—

is not our idea of fun. Most of us like our food long dead and served with a creamy hollandaise and side salad, before meeting it.

Then there are the husbands who like to go home to Mama on their days off, perhaps hoping to get out of laundry duty, in a nostalgic throwback to their college days. So a basic ground rule we established early on was that visits to family members—which, in our case, involved long and stressful trips by plane or vehicle—are not vacations. They are family time, and there's a very big difference. Family time is important, of course. It can even be enjoyable (provided certain relatives are not involved). But just like quality time, family time is not vacation (even if we have to use vacation days to take it). Somehow, you have to figure out how to do both.

I personally recommend training your parents to come to you, but until you have children, this can be difficult. They may be retired, with nothing but time and nest-egg money on their hands, but for some reason, most parents expect their overworked, stressed-out kids to pack up and come to them on their rare days off, instead of them swinging by to visit during one of their many jaunts around the country. I know newlyweds who flat out refuse, but that takes some serious resilience—at least enough to spend the holidays alone,[63] until the parents finally accept that until they get off their retired patooties and come to you, it just ain't happening.

Finally, let's not forget those considerate husbands who insist on quality time NO MATTER WHAT—such as when their wives are minutes away from giving birth to their offspring. One husband we know insisted that his wife, who just happened to be in her third trimester, go camping with him. Maybe the fact that he is an ob-gyn made him a little blasé about the whole process? We're just not sure. Fortunately, he finally agreed to let her stay

---

[63]Not necessarily a bad thing.

home. More fortunate still, for him, is the fact that he made it home before she went into labor.

Another husband—and I really should name names here—insisted that his heavily pregnant wife accompany him on a cross-country car trip. It was winter, and they were moving from one coast to another, passing through snow-filled states. She was less than four weeks from her due date and dilated three full centimeters at the time, and her doctor strongly recommended against it. Not only that, but the husband's company was willing to pay for her plane ticket. The husband, however, didn't want to "be alone" for the trip. Bless his heart.

Questionable Vacation Destinations
- **Booger Holler Trading Post in Dover, Arkansas**—home of the world's only double-decker outhouse (and famous Boogerburger).
- **Gatorland in Kissimmee, Florida**—home of the Gator Jumparoo Show, where fifteen-foot alligators high-jump for chicken carcasses.
- **Ansted, West Virginia**—home of the Mystery Hole, where the laws of nature are reputed to be mysteriously defied, allowing balls to roll uphill.
- **Holly Springs, Mississippi**—home of Graceland Too, an all-pink homage to Elvis and his famous home.
- **Marionville, Missouri**—home of the largest and oldest colony of albino squirrels in the world (estimated to number between three hundred and six hundred).
- **Winston-Salem, North Carolina**—home of the shell-shaped gas station (nonworking).

Questionable Religious Destinations

- **Eureka Springs, Arkansas**—home of the world's tallest uncrucified Christ (seven stories high, two million pounds).
- **Cassadaga, Florida**—psychic center of the world and home to a colony of spiritualists.
- **Monroe, Ohio**—home of a giant Jesus sculpture standing sixty-two feet tall, appearing to rise (waist up only) from the baptismal pool of Solid Rock Church.
- **Tulsa, Oklahoma**—home of the Healing Hands, a forty-foot-tall bronze statue at the entrance to Oral Roberts University.
- **Field of the Wood in Murphy, North Carolina**—home of the world's largest Ten Commandments, a three-hundred-foot-wide tableaux carved into the mountainside facing Prayer Mountain.
- **Dry Rocks Reef off Key Largo, Florida**—home of Christ of the Deep, a nine-foot-tall bronze statue located twenty-five feet underwater.

No matter where you're going, however—even if it's Dry Rocks Reef off of Key Largo, twenty-five feet below—you will definitely need to stock up on maps and directions. After all, you will not be asking for directions under any circumstances, no matter how much you might beg or how lost you may get. Anthropologists are still trying to figure out why men will drive 250 miles out of their way rather than ask for help from a prepubescent gas station attendant they'll never set eyes on again.

In my not-so-humble opinion, there is only one way to solve this problem, and that's by joining an auto club like AAA. In addition to using their full-scale travel agency, you can map out car trips mile by mile (including hotels, restaurants, attractions and even gas stations), using their "TripTik" service. They'll even mail you free, state-by-state TourBooks, which contain historical overviews of every city and town as well as detailed summaries of existing accommodations, restaurants and attractions. We never go anywhere without them, in fact. The best part, however, is their free roadside service for repairs, flat tires, gas and locksmiths, which has saved us from many a marital dispute. Not that I would ever run out of gas or lock myself out of the car, mind you. Nah.

Finally, beware the idiosyncrasies of men, when traveling—which you probably won't ever be able to change. My husband will drive ten miles out of the way just to get to a gas station he likes. Recently, before leaving town for a long trip, he insisted on driving out of our way for a particular station just so he could buy some oil and put air in the tires.

"But we're going to be passing at least fifteen gas stations on the way," I said, trying to deter him. "And we're already an hour late."

"No, I like this one," he said.

"Please. We're going to catch all those lights. Let's just go to one along the way. They're gas stations—they all have air and oil."

"No, they don't. Only some have air," he argued, bypassing the entrance ramp for the freeway and heading toward "his" station.

"All gas stations have air!"

"No, they don't," he said. "And even if they do, they're not always working. At least I know this one is working. I was there last week."

We pulled in, and guess what. The air machine wasn't working. But even though we were about to head for another station, Mark still insisted on going in and purchasing oil at that station.

"It's better here," he said.

NINE

Socializing and Entertaining: Oh, Babe, What Would You Say?

T he art of socializing—otherwise known as how to make, keep and not embarrass yourself in front of friends—is hugely important for newlyweds. After all, if you don't have any friends, what will you do on Super Bowl Sunday?

Now I truly do not know why this is, but socially speaking, getting married has a way of bringing out the beast in men. Honestly, you take a bachelor who wouldn't dream of cracking his knuckles in front of the dog, put a wedding ring on the man and he's playing the fiddle with his fanny[64] at your mother's birthday party. I figure this must be instinctive—kind of like the way we ladies suck in our guts at the beach, then hit the water and breathe.

---

[64]Otherwise known as "tooting."

So all I can say is, you may want to prepare yourself for the occasional embarrassment.

Like many Southern Girls, I grew up under the tutelage of a mother obsessed with etiquette. Manners weren't simply adhered to in our house. They were drilled into us with the regularity of a metronome. We kept napkins on our laps, elbows off the table and utensils in their proper places. We made polite conversation, didn't interrupt and always asked before leaving the table. And every meal was eaten on fine china and with silver—even if we were having hamburgers.

This has served me well for black-tie dinners, where I'm at ease with a zillion forks and the proper way to eat that last bit of soup (tilt the bowl away from you). Alas, I don't get to use this training very often because formal entertaining, it appears, has gone the way of Farrah haircuts. I'm not even that old, either—just Southern. Which means that I possess a host of expectations that are dashed each and every day in a world that is becoming increasingly un-Southern.

Take doors, for instance. Where I was growing up, men opened them for women. Contrary to what some women believe, this little courtesy never made me feel inferior. Opening doors was and is an issue of social propriety, a code of honor that men, especially Southern Boys, used to stick to like honey on the kitchen floor. And thankfully, many still do.[65] But sadly, there are so many other men out there doing just the opposite that entering and exiting the Harris Teeter (or "Harris-n-Teeter," as we like to say) is like trying to cross I-95 at rush hour. Most days I'm lucky if I can get through a set of double doors without being trampled. And I won't even raise the subject of parking lots, where I've had more than a few "gentlemen" just about total my car in a bid to grab the

---

[65]Same thing in the military, where men not only open doors for you but call you "ma' am," as well. It's positively refreshing, I tell you.

closest spot. So let's just say that chivalry is dead and Bill Clinton likes sex—and neither is breaking news.

When it comes to marriage, however, these issues take on the importance of a head count to a caterer. You and your new husband will want to entertain and be entertained, and it can feel an awful lot like you're onstage, especially during those early months. You are, in fact. But so is everyone else. And the goal is not to out-perform one another. It's to get invited back.

Nowadays, my husband behaves rather well in front of guests. Early on in our marriage, however, you never knew what he might do. I refer, in particular, to the Incident of the Roast Beef.

Still graduate students, Mark and I were living on a very tight budget. We were therefore looking forward to a dinner party one Saturday evening, when I planned on serving a large roast beef. It wasn't every day that we ate expensive cuts of meat, after all (Mark's breakfast tendencies notwithstanding). So I spent most of the day cooking, setting the table and getting dressed, while the beef simmered in the oven, surrounded by buttered carrots, potatoes and parsnips and a sprinkling of fresh thyme.

After our guests arrived, we enjoyed hors d'oeuvres and cocktails in the living room. Everyone then moved to the table for the first course. For the entrée, I extracted the beef from the oven and transferred everything to the china serving platter (a wedding gift). I then brought it all to the table. With a flourish, I handed Mark the carving tools and asked him to do the honors.

When I returned to the dining room, after whisking together the gravy in the kitchen, a distinct awkwardness had settled over the table. One of the women was biting her lip. Another was looking at the floor. The third had a fake smile plastered to her face. The men, however, were chatting with Mark, oblivious to their wives' dismay. I glanced under the table, looking for a broken dish. Nothing but vacuum tracks. On the table were one, two, three . . . eight wineglasses, all sitting upright. No stains on the tablecloth, either. Nothing, in fact, appeared to be amiss.

Then I saw the serving platter. What had once been a perfectly seasoned, stunning roast was now a stew. Instead of slicing that beef, my new husband had diced it—all ten pounds of it—into tiny, one-inch squares. And I regret to say that I did not appreciate the humor of the situation one tiny, little bit. At least we had a nice dessert.

Here's the recipe for the pecan pie that I served for dessert that night. It remained intact, by the way. It's from my aunt Nancy, and like many Southerners, we eat it every year for Thanksgiving— instead of pumpkin pie. I firmly believe that every Southern Girl should know how to make a pecan pie, and thankfully, it's as easy as you please. In fact, this pie will be one of the easiest things you've ever made, and you'll get so many compliments you'll feel just like Paula Deen.[66] Watch out, though. It's addictive!

Aunt Nancy's Pecan Pie

3 eggs, slightly beaten
½ cup sugar
4 tablespoons melted butter
1 cup Karo syrup (I use ½ light and ½ dark)
1 cup whole pecans
1 teaspoon vanilla

1. Mix all ingredients in order and pour into unbaked 9-inch pie shell (the refrigerated kind that you unroll will work

[66]Don't you just love her?

fine—it's right next to the prepared cookie dough in the refrigerator section).

2. Bake 10 minutes at 450° F, then 35 minutes at 300° F.

3. Let cool and serve with vanilla ice cream.

Note: Do not double this recipe. If you do, it will look fine on top (because the pecans rise) but when you cut it, everything will just run out. So, if you want more, you have to make 2 pies!

Now there are some truly scary social habits out there, and I'm not talking about dicing meat—or even the inability to write thank-you notes, as frightening as that is. I'm talking about things that make you realize exactly why formal entertaining died a slow and agonizing death. Things like reaching across plates (or the entire table) for the salt shaker, or a guest pouring himself more wine, without waiting for the host. Or how about chewing and talking with open mouths, as if people somehow enjoy the sight of masticated food? I often think of that childhood rhyme, "Annabelle, Annabelle, strong and able, keep your elbows off the table," and unwittingly make up new ones, like "Bubba, Bubba, don't be a hick. Floss in your bathroom, not with a toothpick."

Years ago, I was at a party when a husband had far too much to drink and started telling off-color jokes. Now I don't know about elsewhere, but in the South this is a cardinal sin. Men barely even cuss in front of a woman, if they're raised right. It was embarrassing, to say the least, and we all felt sorry for his wife, who couldn't get him to stop. I tell you, the wives of drunk husbands could probably write a book on embarrassing moments.

And then there are the geeks. One Southern Girl shared that

her husband likes to sing out loud to the music—not just at parties, but also in elevators, grocery stores and even waiting rooms. Remember Elaine's little leg-thrusting dance on *Seinfeld*? Another Southern Girl said that her husband dances exactly like that, every time they hit the floor. Of course, this is only slightly better than the husband who "hand dances" from the sofa whenever the music comes on at someone's house.

Mark and I once attended an engagement party for a coworker. Her fiancé was a really nice guy, very attractive, with a sense of humor. Unfortunately, however, his humor came straight from *Reader's Digest* magazine. I don't mean "inspired by" *Reader's Digest*. I mean, word for word, from the current issue. Now I love *Reader's Digest*. I read it all the time and have since I was a kid. I even mouthed off to my grandmother once when I was fourteen in what became an oft-repeated line. For some bizarre reason, she asked if I was using drugs. Huh? Drugs? Uh, did I look like a stoner? Raised Ralph Lauren collar? Pink-and-green purse? Tretorn tennis shoes? Hello! I had my issues as a teenager, but drugs were not one of them.

"Well!" said my grandmother, as only she could, packing a dozen meanings into a word and a raised eyebrow. "I know all about drugs, and it's an issue with kids today!" I shook my head and said, with no small amount of impertinence, "Marmee, the only thing you know about teenagers is what you read in *Reader's Digest*!"

So I'm a longtime fan of *Reader's Digest*. But unfortunately, this gal's fiancé was, too—and I mean a real fan. And maybe there weren't many *Reader's Digest* readers present that night, or maybe they had yet to read their copy, but I couldn't have been the only one who knew all the punch lines. My smile was so frozen, I felt like a beauty contestant who'd forgotten to Vaseline her teeth.

A very charming Southern Girl I know is married to a Yankee who used to own a junk shop up North. The daughter of a dignitary, she grew up attending black-tie functions. He grew up in a small-town, blue-collar family of simple means (but oh, can this man cook). So you can imagine her embarrassment when she discovered that her stunningly handsome husband enjoyed scavenging roadside debris. Whenever he discovers a "find" inside the neighbor's trash, he just wanders over and inspects it. And he won't hesitate to stop their car and load up an item that he's spotted while they're out for a drive, either. All she can do is close her eyes and pray that no one they know is nearby.[67]

At social events, all of your husband's eccentricities will be on display—everything from his penchant for tacky clothing to his insistence on debating politics, race and religion with politicians, clergy and people of other races. For some men, a rousing debate is the civilized equivalent of a barroom brawl, but it tends to leave most wives cringing. The most embarrassing things husbands do out in public, however, usually have to do with . . . well . . . shall we say, bodily functions. I really don't want to go into details, but I mean anything and everything, and just imagine your husband doing them in front of friends and family.

Therefore, whether entertaining or being entertained, trust me when I say that it can be most helpful to establish a few ground rules. Yes, you can try and explain protocol to your husband. But, unless he was raised in a swamp, he's already heard it all before. The problem isn't that men don't know what to do—it's that they don't listen. And even when they do, there's always the issue of short-term memory, which a startling percentage of men seem to lack. Never fear, however,

---

[67]In some ways, it's better than a yard sale, I guess. No competition at least.

because there is one situation when men pay rapt attention and remember exactly what they are told. It is to this situation that we now turn our attention.

War

When it comes to getting a man to listen, I have found anything to do with the military to be extremely effective. Remember that scene early in *Gone With the Wind*, when Scarlett is sitting among a bevy of young suitors? None of the other belles can get any attention. But as soon as the boys hear the South has seceded, poor Scarlett is forgotten, too.

The reason for this fascination, I suspect, is genetic imprinting. Men have been making war, after all, since the beginning of time. Either that, or they just like pretending they're eight years old again, playing in the backyard. So, given the foreign nature of social events for many men, I suggest staging something the military calls a "Predeployment Line Briefing," or "PDL." Held immediately before troops head overseas, PDLs provide them with everything they need to know in order to accomplish their strategic objectives and return safely.

During a PDL, a soldier receives a series of information categorized into briefings. The "mission briefing," for example, reminds a man of the mission's goals, as well as his target and objectives. In the "cultural briefing," a soldier learns how to interact with—and not offend—the alien culture. An "intelligence briefing" reviews what he needs to know about the enemy and any hostile threats he may face while deployed. In the "health briefing," he hears about necessary precautions he must take for safeguarding his physical well-being. The "religious briefing" provides guidelines for practicing his faith, and the "Law of Armed Conflict (LOAC) briefing" is a brief review about the rules of engagement so necessary for a successful military campaign.

Prior to your social event, therefore, schedule a predeployment briefing with your husband. That way, if he is in the military, he will be able to relate to the concepts and you will have his rapt attention. And if he's not in the military, it will allow him to pretend like he is.

Sample Predeployment Briefing: Cousin Julie's Wedding

1. MISSION BRIEFING

Mission Goal: Attend Julie's wedding, go through receiving line and attend reception, while I (your wife) carry out my bridesmaid responsibilities nearby (but watch your every move).

Mission Target: All Soul's Church, 503 Juniper Drive (located just around the corner from our house, but see attached map, globe, atlas, global-position device and detailed driving directions from four different Internet sites, just in case).

Mission Objectives: a) Arrive on time for ceremony.
b) Remain awake during ceremony.

    c) Congratulate couple during receiving line, without alluding to bride's past.

    d) Talk to people other than your best friend.

2. CULTURAL BRIEFING

Alien Culture: Episcopalians

Interaction Guidelines: a) Dress conservatively, in dark colors. Episcopalians do not like color or creativity from their men. Do not forget underwear.

    b) Be prepared to stand and sit until legs are sore. Episcopalians are notoriously energetic worshippers.

    c) Follow wedding program throughout ceremony without any emotion or facial expression. Otherwise the Episcopalians will think you are Pentecostal and become frightened.

    d) Move quickly through receiving line. It matters little what you say, because no one is listening. However, do not engage in postgame analysis while shaking hands, as that will delay the wait for the bar and make Episcopalians very angry.

Offensive Actions: a) Burping, passing gas or engaging
in any bodily function (including
breathing) during ceremony.
b) Objecting when rectors asks
congregation for objections.
c) Overfilling plate at buffet.
d) Eating dessert (wedding cake)
before being cut by bride and
groom.

3. INTELLIGENCE BRIEFING

Suspicious Characters: My father
Hostile Threats: My mother
Enemy Agents: My ex-boyfriend (Robert,
Groomsman No. 3—the one who
looks like a bodybuilder. He is.)

4. HEALTH BRIEFING

a) Do not get drunk.
b) Do not fall asleep.
c) Do not eat the deviled eggs prepared by Great-aunt Mary
(the ones covered in dog hair).
d) Do not ask rector about theology of birth control.

5. RELIGIOUS BRIEFING (HOLY EUCHARIST)

a) Go to front of church when poked by neighbor.
b) Kneel at communion bench.
c) Sip, do not gulp, communion cup.

d) Do not talk with mouth full.

e) Do not ask for seconds.

LOAC BRIEFING (RULES OF ENGAGEMENT)

a) Don't challenge Robert to a fight. He will beat you up.

b) Don't argue with Mother. She will beat you up.

c) Don't dive for the bouquet. The single women will beat you up.

Keep Your Hands to Yourself

In addition to briefing your husband prior to any social event, you will also want to maintain close watch during the event itself. Particularly during the early months after your wedding, do not assume anything—no matter how courteous your beau may have been while dating. It may be years since he's gatored or fountain hopped, but the curious combination of friends and alcohol has a way of taking a man straight back to the fraternity house.

I also suggest that you develop a set of flash cards. Remember the ones your mother used when you were in the fourth grade to help you memorize your multiplication tables?[68] Well, your cards will need to be slightly bigger so your husband can see them from the other side of the room, where you will be discreetly flashing them. Blank note cards and Popsicle sticks should do the trick, though. Just write out your messages ahead of time, one on each side, then glue two of them together, facing out, with the stick in

---

[68] I think I need to review those, actually.

the middle. Be sure to buy a new purse large enough to hold them all. Prada makes a very good one. So does Kate Spade. Coach, too. But don't limit yourself. Shop around.

Here are some suggested phrases you can employ on your cards, but think creatively. It's unfortunate, but every husband has different issues, so the list of habits that need curtailing could be endless. Also, don't forget to bring a few blank cards whenever you go out—for those unexpected little etiquette emergencies. Finally, consider storing your flash cards in the car. That way, you'll always have them on hand for impromptu social events. Not only that, but you can use them on other drivers. In fact, as long as you're going to the trouble, you might just go ahead and make driving-specific flash cards. You know, phrases like "Blinker!" or "Rearview mirror!" After all, those rude male drivers are married to somebody, right? You just might be doing their wives a favor.

Suggested Phrases for Social Flash Cards

No/Yes

Laugh/Don't laugh

Answer/Don't answer

Look interested/Look sad

Say something/Shhhhh

Stop staring/Stop glaring

Stop eating/Stop drinking

Stop scratching/Start backpedaling

You're snorting/You're snoring

The Good, the Bad and the Ugly

Clothing is the final frontier when it comes to husbands and social engagements. It can either make you or break you in the social arena. And if you don't believe me, I have one word for you: Speedo.

My daddy used to have a tie collection that he'd trot out for special occasions, and God bless my stepmother for putting up with 'em. For some strange reason, Southern Boys just love to pretend they're rednecks, even if the closest they've ever come to a trailer park is driving past one en route to their beach house. Daddy was no exception, and toward this end, he had a Rudolph tie for Christmas, a turkey tie for Thanksgiving, and the ubiquitous rebel flag tie. His favorite, however, was covered in pigs holding signs that said "MCP," for "male chauvinist pig." Now I think that qualifies as a 10 on the cringe factor, don't you?

According to my brother Stephen, a former Brooks Brothers store manager, Daddy is in good company. Most men, he says, own at least one item of clothing that is very ugly and very embarrassing. It might even smell, Stephen says. Men know this, but they nevertheless feel really cool wearing their particular item. Mark's is a pair of shoes that look like they came from a Tijuana yard sale. He swears they are the most comfortable pair he's ever worn—and maybe they are, but they make me want to crawl under the nearest picnic table.

Actually, Mark has excellent taste in clothes. He's even drifting away from the four colors that used to define his entire wardrobe (dark blue, dark green, gray and khaki.) I actually got him to wear a pink tie for Easter this year, and everyone agreed he looked fabulous. If he were Southern, of course, he'd have been wearing pastels for years. Even the most conservative Southern

Boy enjoys a little color every now and then—especially on the golf course, where things can get extremely loud. Pink, green and orange plaid, anyone?

Mark says men have it easy when it comes to clothes; they only need to choose a tie. But, oh, honey. This assumes that all men dress alike, and unfortunately, my preppy husband doesn't realize just how creative men can be when it comes to clothing. As in the prison wear that's all the rage right now (baggy pants, untied shoes, knit hats). So, in view of this alarming trend, I thought it might be helpful to ask Stephen for a little advice. Because if anyone knows fashion, it's Brooks Brothers.[69]

Remember, just because an outfit worked fifteen years ago doesn't mean it still looks good. Men's fashion may not change dramatically from year to year—and good quality never goes out of style—but styles do change. And occasionally, a man has to change with them. Just make sure to consult an expert before you throw your khakis to the wind.

So first, says Stephen, a man should always wear a T-shirt and button up a dress shirt. Nobody wants to see sweat rings under his arms, and looking at chest hair isn't particularly appealing either.

Second, understand the way socks work (even if the Euro-tourists don't). With suits and trousers, men should wear only dark socks. With shorts, they should wear only white ones. And never—never, ever—should the twain meet.

Third, unless he's the Abercrombie & Fitch model (or Simon Cowell—in which case you have my condolences), please tell your husband to forgo body-hugging T-shirts and sweaters. They do not look sexy; they look stupid. And don't forget a shirt under your sweaters, boys.

---

[69]And if you don't know what Brooks Brothers is, then, darlin', please turn on the computer and Google it as fast as you can—and do consider leaving California.

Finally, the most important rule of all: make sure your clothes fit. Stephen says he is always amazed to see how many men knowingly wear clothing that is way too small for them. "You may have had a thirty-two-inch waist in the Marine Corps, but if it's forty now, you're not fooling anyone by squeezing into a smaller size," he says. "You just look like a frog in trousers."

Brooks Brothers won't even sell a man the wrong size, Stephen says, even if a customer insists. The brand name is far too important for people to walk around looking like they didn't get decent advice. The good news is that this issue hardly ever crops up, because good associates don't need to ask sizes. Most will give a new customer the once-over, then start bringing out clothing— regardless of what size a man says he wears. Stephen glanced at my husband, and even though Mark was wearing a bulky sweater, accurately guessed his neck size, shirt length and waist circumference. I was impressed.

The problem, of course, is that most men have neither the time nor the inclination to shop the way they need to. However, this is why God gave men wives. Just like God gave me an accountant, in the form of a husband. After the wedding, Mark and I didn't even discuss who would pay the bills. Mark said, "See this stick? Receipts go there. Bills go in the drawer. Don't even open them up— just hand 'em over. Now here's your checkbook." Honestly, I thought I had died and gone to heaven. (Love ya, baby.)

Same thing for clothing and men. Women have been dressing them since they were born, anyway, so why fight tradition? All you need to do is find one little hour in his busy schedule. Drop by a store like Brooks Brothers and let them take down his sizes. Then turn the shopping over to the experts. He'll be handsome; you'll be happy. And, as any experienced husband knows, when the wife is happy, the world is happy.

Now, ladies, once you have acquired a new (or updated)

wardrobe for your husband, you're almost ready to take him out in public. If he is capable of matching trousers, shirts, ties, belts, shoes and socks on his own—in other words, if he is a Rubik's Cube champion—you're home free. Get dressed and go party. Otherwise, your work is not quite complete.

Lions and Tigers and Bears . . . Oh, My!

Your final mission, should you choose to accept it, is to come up with a system that enables your husband to get dressed all by himself. Yes, all things are possible for those who believe. Remember Garanimals? A great idea for little boys, an even better idea for big boys.

Now Garanimals, you may recall, uses labels printed with animals—lions, giraffes, chimps and so forth. All the Garanimals pants and shorts with a panda label, for example, match the Garanimals shirts with a panda label. The jaguar pants and shorts match the jaguar shirts, and so on. Simple, no? All a kid has to do is pick a pair of pants, examine the label and find a shirt with the same label, and voilà! He matches.

Since you can't create labels from scratch (who creates anything from scratch nowadays?), try and find patches instead. Buy ones that are small enough to iron onto clothing tags, and buy three or four different sets. Stick to a theme like sports and purchase a dozen football patches, a dozen baseball patches, a dozen basketball ones and so forth. Then go to work matching and ironing.[70]

If you don't like the patch idea, you can always draw symbols

---

[70]Speaking of ironing (particularly if you're stuck with this chore) and Brooks Brothers, you may want to check out their new, noniron dress shirts. They're not cheap, but they're gorgeous, and those suckers come out of the dryer looking like they've done hard time at the cleaners.

on his tags. But no matter which system you go for, make sure all his tags are tucked in before he leaves the house.

You Don't Bring Me Flowers

Finally, before engaging in any social activities, you will definitely want to assess the hospitality quotient of your guests. By this, I mean that you should try and determine whether your guests (or hosts) have a clue about entertaining, particularly if you live outside the South and/or socialize with non-Southerners. Otherwise, the evening could end in disaster, and it won't have a thing to do with your husband. You see, as a good Southern Girl, you will want to meet—but not overpower—people's expectations. And trust me when I say that people have very different attitudes about socializing. These attitudes are influenced by cultural, geographical and socioeconomic backgrounds, as well as their own emotional issues. In other words, some people are just plain rude.

Early on in our marriage, I made the mistake of pulling out all the stops when it came to dinner parties. I cooked, I set out fine china, I served multiple courses. I thought I was merely entertaining, and for most people, I was. But I now know that occasionally someone felt just a wee bit overwhelmed. Most people spent the evening with us, called the next day to say thanks (known in the South as a "bread-and-butter call") and then, a few weeks later, reciprocated by inviting us over. But every now and then, one of our guests would just disappear, never to be heard from again.

Needless to say, we were confused. But then, a non-Southern guest started blathering about being "completely unable to reciprocate," and I realized the problem. We weren't in the South. And while most people adapt to good hospitality no matter where they live, this sort of entertaining simply wasn't commonplace anymore.

We had, to quote an old cliché, been killing people with kindness. Southern kindness.

So before you set the table with linen napkins and call the caterer, think about the last time you saw your hosts or guests. How do they dress? What are their favorite restaurants? What hangs on their walls? If it's quilts and life-sized family photos, a pig pickin' will probably work. If it's a signed Georgia O'Keeffe, the caterer might be a good idea.

Also, be sure to ask any hostess—as in, the woman of the house—about the nature of any event you are invited to. Husbands are not particularly reliable when it comes to information transmission (remember Adam in the Garden). I often receive invitations for upcoming baby showers, weddings and parties that Mark has passed on to me from a hostess. The only problem is, like many husbands, he typically gives them to me the day of the event or after they're over. And for heaven's sakes, don't let your husband issue any invitations before checking with you. Otherwise, you may find yourself trying to disguise General Tsao's chicken as something you "just whipped up."[71]

Even if your husband does give you an invitation on time, however, you must avoid asking him about the dress code. In fact, it's better to avoid asking any man at all about what to wear. And by this, I do not mean, "Honey, should I wear the red dress or the black dress?" I'm talking, "Is this black tie or beachwear?"

We recently attended a formal military ball. Unfortunately, we didn't know it was a formal event, because the commander of the host squadron—great guy, just a little clueless on the fashion front—told Mark it was casual. When we arrived, most of the women (including his own wife), were wearing floor-length ball

---

[71]This, by the way, is why it's oh so important to have good china and serving dishes.

gowns. Fortunately, I had worn a dressy casual outfit, just in case. But I still felt like a straight guy at a hairdresser's convention.

Another time, we attended a dinner party at the home of Mark's new boss. We had been told that all of Mark's new superiors and colleagues would be present, so we brought flowers and dressed up. Unfortunately, as soon as we walked through the door, I realized our faux pas. Not only were we the only ones to bring a hostess gift, but we had missed the social mark by a mile. I had fortunately bypassed a skirt, high heels and pearls for linen pants and sandals. But you can still imagine my embarrassment when I saw the other couples in sweatshirts and old jeans. The host was actually barefoot and in running shorts—and it was chilly outside.

Needless to say, Southerners don't dress like this for any social event, but certainly not for dinner parties where they're scheduled to meet their new bosses.[72] The meal was just as casual, too, with do-it-yourself sandwiches eaten in the kitchen. As if that's not enough, twenty minutes after dinner, the boss was also sprawled on the floor, engrossed in a video game, while his wife talked on the phone with friends. As we sat on the sofa, watching this scenario, we couldn't help but wonder if we had mistakenly invited ourselves over.

Moral of the story? When attending an event, do your homework, then prepare accordingly. After all, you never know when it's your hosts—and not your husband—who will embarrass you most.

---

[72]Unless the boss happens to be their new track coach, of course.

TEN

The Mother-in-Law: I Wanna Be Sedated

A long time ago, in a faraway land, two mothers came before a king, dragging a young woman between them. "My lord, this girl is betrothed to my son," said the first. The other said, "No! It is my son she is to marry."

The women argued until the king silenced them. "One of you says that she is to be your daughter-in-law. Then the other one says that she is to be your daughter-in-law," he said. "Now bring me my sword!"

The servants brought the sword to the king, who gave the order, "Cut this girl in two. Give half to one and half to the other."

The first mother cried, "Please, my lord, give her the girl! Don't kill her!"

The second said, "Neither you nor I shall have her. Cut her in two!"

"Give the girl to the second woman," said the king.

"The second woman!" cried the astonished court. "But she would see the girl hewn in two."

"Yes," answered the wise king. "This shows that she is her true mother-in-law."

Now, for some reason, fathers-in-law don't seem to cause too many problems when a couple marries—although my daddy did make quite the impression on Mark, the first time we went to visit. After picking us up at the Raleigh-Durham airport, he ushered us to his car—a Lincoln Continental with a bumper sticker that read, *On the 8th Day, God Created Marines*. Before sliding behind the wheel, Daddy—who happens to be a murder defense attorney and who is therefore maybe just a little bit paranoid—reached into his belt and pulled out a large handgun, which he placed on the dashboard. As we drove home, the gun slid back and forth across the dash. To the right, when we made a left turn. To the left, when we made a right turn.

"Uh, Carl? Why do you have a gun on the dashboard?" Mark said finally, his eyes wide.

"It's illegal to carry a concealed weapon," my father answered, in his slow Southern drawl.

As if that wasn't enough to put fear into the heart of a new husband, once we got home, Daddy put the gun on the coffee table, right next to the channel changer. Mark later said that he was terrified my father would mistake the gun for the remote and accidentally shoot him.

Mothers-in-law are a whole different ball game. The very word strikes fear into the soul of any bride with a soul. And if you don't believe me, try scrambling it. Think it's a coincidence that you can spell "Woman Hitler?" Then why does Mother-in-Law Day fall just a few days before Halloween? As my husband says, is this a day of celebration or mourning?

But surely, you say, your husband's mother will be different. She bore him, she raised him, she adores him. She wants to see her dear son happy. And who could possibly deny that you are the one who makes that man happy?

Oh, darlin'. You better sit down. Would you like some coffee? Some sweet tea? Some valium?

There now, where do I start . . . ? Well how about the cliché? Because clichés are clichés for a reason, you see. They're clichés because they happen over and over again. They're clichés because everyone can relate to them. And if everyone can relate to feelings of abhorrence, aggravation, anger, annoyance, antagonism, anxiety, apprehension—wait, I'm just in the "As." I'd better slow down. But do you get what I'm saying? We're talking emotions, honey. Big ones. The whole alphabet of negative feelings.

Am I exaggerating?[73] Of course. At least for some of you, and even myself, because I have great in-laws. My biggest regret is that we don't see them more often. Honestly. So it can and does happen. However, I do realize that saying this to most brides is a bit like telling your best friend that you're wearing a size 2, when she'd be doing backflips to squeeze into a 16. So please accept my apologies, and I promise not to belabor the point. In the meantime, there are more than enough horror stories to go around.

[73]Who, me?

Daughter-in-Law Survival Kit

- New Locks—for doors
- Caller ID—for phones
- Duct Tape—for mouth
- Earplugs (2)—for arguments
- Tape recorder—for evidence
- Wig and sunglasses—for gatherings

Hit Me With Your Best Shot

Mothers-in-law are often critical of their sons' wives. It's as if somehow, instead of a sign saying JUST MARRIED on the back of your car, when you drive away from the wedding, someone spray-painted OPEN SEASON instead. No matter how normal their in-laws may be, most Southern Girls have experienced at least one or two tactless comments. Interestingly enough, these "observations" frequently have to do with cleaning, which seems to be a very sticky subject indeed.

One of my mothers-in-law[74] was a scientist we enjoyed spending time with. She helped around the house, was a great conversationalist and the most devoted grandmother you could possibly imagine. She could sometimes be insensitive, though. So, when I realized that cleanliness was definitely next to godliness for her, I made sure that my house was spotless. On one particular occasion, I left her with my daughter to attend a conference. As my

[74]Multiple mothers-in-law: one of the many legacies of the baby boomers.

plane taxied down the runway, I suddenly had a sinking feeling. I had forgotten to dust the ceiling fan. I'd been meaning to clean it, but working from home with a toddler has a tendency to waylay even the best-laid plans of mothers. Dang it. Hopefully, she wouldn't notice.

After I got home, I was not surprised to hear her say that she had done some cleaning.

"I'm sorry," I said, cringing. "I thought I had left the house clean." Then I glanced up at the ceiling fan. It had, of course, been dusted.

"Oh, don't worry," she replied. "It's something that would never even occur to you to clean."

Other mothers-in-law are far more direct. One Southern Girl said that every time her mother-in-law arrived for a visit, she would put down her suitcase and grab a mop. Nothing could dissuade the mother-in-law from scrubbing her room and bathroom—even when the couple began hiring professional cleaners before her visits.

"Everyone has different standards of cleanliness," she would say with a sniff.

This same mother-in-law would also clean directly behind her daughter-in-law, sometimes even taking dishes out of the dishwasher to scrub just minutes after the daughter-in-law had put them in. The daughter-in-law could barely lift a sponge, she said, before her mother-in-law was wiping down the counter behind her.

Many Southern Girls recalled criticism about their cooking. "You call this a meal?" said one mother-in-law before halfheartedly adding, "Just kidding."

Others take over, cooking meals before anyone else can get into the kitchen. The only problem with that, said one Southern Girl, is the mother-in-law's constant comments about how inept "young girls" were in the kitchen "today."

"How original" was the icy refrain of another mother-in-law

whenever she tasted her daughter-in-law's cuisine. Instead of eating that "original" meal, however, she would go into the kitchen, make herself a sandwich and return to the dining room to eat.

My sister's mother-in-law implied all sorts of doom and gloom when she learned that my sister's spaghetti sauce wasn't homemade. She did everything she could to persuade her to throw it out and make a new one from scratch, right then and there. "It's just not good for you," she said finally, eyeing the Ragu like a jarful of botulism. After dinner, she went out and bought a three-month supply of tomatoes. Or, to be precise, she instructed her son to take her to the store, where she picked out the tomatoes for him to buy.

Several Southern Girls shared comments that their mothers-in-law had made about their personal habits—everything from drinking and smoking to even working out "too much." One lamented that her mother-in-law never lost the chance to remind her to put on more makeup.

"You can't let yourself go," she would warn, obviously forgetting that she was talking about her own son. "A husband will stray."

Sometimes, it seems, mothers-in-law are just looking for an excuse to argue. One Southern Girl told how she had bought a new bed specifically for the mother-in-law's visit. Being newly married, they did not have a lot of money, but because the mother-in-law was critical, they purchased a quality mattress set and made sure to tell her. The morning after her arrival, however, she came into the kitchen grimacing.

"That's the worst night's sleep I've ever had," she said. "I don't see how that mattress could be new. You must have pulled it out of the Dumpster."

When the daughter-in-law offered to show her the receipt, the mother-in-law shook her head. "That's impossible. This thing couldn't have come from anywhere but the Salvation Army."

Devil Woman

For some reason, gifts also tend to be a huge issue with mothers-in-law, who like to communicate through this medium. Unfortunately, however, their message seems to be about tacky and cheap things, because that's what many of their gifts are.

Tacky Mother-in-Law Gift Hall of Fame

- Ab machine and one-year membership to Weight Watchers
- Diet books and/or diet pills
- A full year's worth of chocolate, delivered once a month (for dieting daughter-in-law)
- Red plastic purse, on sale at Wal-mart (sales tag still attached)
- Coffee mug filled with candy (every year for Christmas)
- Anything from a garage sale or thrift store, if attempted to be passed off as new
- Two-week luxury vacation to Hawaii (for mother-in-law and son to enjoy alone)

Every Christmas, one Southern Girl receives a candy-filled mug—a regular old coffee mug full of Brach's peppermints—from her well-to-do mother-in-law. Meanwhile, beside her, her husband is opening box after box of expensive clothing. Another Southern Girl once received a red plastic purse from her mother-in-law, an attorney with a six-figure income who wears nothing but designer labels. The purse still had the tag showing that it had come from Wal-Mart. It had been marked down.

More than one Southern Girl said that she had received used gifts from her mother-in-law, even for Christmas and birthdays. Although some were offended, those who regularly peruse thrift stores and garage sales were more blasé. Their biggest problem was the fact that the mothers-in-law tried to pass off the gifts as new.

"If they would just say, 'Hey, I found this while thrifting and thought you'd like it,'" said one, "I'd be fine. But to go on and on about how she searched for it all day in the mall, when the thing is obviously ten years old and falling apart, is just plain ridiculous."

Regifting is also common. A few Southern Girls have received gifts that they know were given to their mothers-in-law first. In one case, the mother-in-law opened a Christmas present in front of the entire family, then wrapped it up and regifted it to the daughter-in-law a few days later, for her birthday, in front of the same family members.

"Does she think I'm blind?" said the daughter-in-law. "Or stupid?"

Another mother-in-law actually had the audacity to return the same gift her daughter-in-law had given her. She didn't just give it back, though. She waited until Christmas, when everyone was watching, then handed it to her.

"For once in my life, I was speechless," said the daughter-in-law. "I had gone to a lot of trouble of making her a huge basket of specialty coffees, which she claimed to adore, with lots of coffee-related items, like china cups, flavored syrups and chocolate-covered coffee beans. The main part of the gift was a French press, which she'd been saying she wanted for months. Naturally, that was missing. But everything else was right there in the basket, where I had put it."

Some time after the wedding, many brides find themselves facing—and trying to lose—the dreaded "newlywed nineteen." So they go on a diet, telling everyone in the family that they need support, and begin working out. That's when the mother-in-law arrives, in time to sabotage any progress. Many dieting daughters-in-law reported receiving chocolate, candy, cookies and cakes during this time—when they had never been given such a gift before. One received a full year of her favorite chocolate, with a basket of the sweets scheduled to arrive each and every month thereafter.

Instead of destroying diet plans, other mothers-in-law prefer to humiliate their sons' wives by giving them a gift that tells them they're fat—whether they are or not. Several Southern Girls said that they had received diet books from their mothers-in-laws. One received an ab machine and a year's membership to Weight Watchers. Still another received a gift basket full of diet pills, in front of all her friends and family. She was so embarrassed that she burst into tears.

"It's okay, dear," said the mother-in-law, patting her hand. "If you'll just focus, you'll get thin. Someday."

Occasionally, mothers-in-law give gifts to their sons with an underlying message for the daughter-in-law. One mother gave her son a book about living with a dysfunctional wife. "I wanted to ask if her husband had read it first," quipped the daughter-in-law.

Another gave her son a fully paid, two-week luxury vacation for two to Hawaii—with her. When the wife protested, her mother-in-law batted her eyes and said, "You have him all to yourself fifty weeks of the year, yet you begrudge me two weeks alone with my only son?"

Perhaps the worst story is the one about the mother who gave her son one of those I'M WITH STUPID T-shirts, a few months after the wedding. Fortunately, the daughter-in-law, who had been taunted by snotty comments from the mother-in-law throughout their courtship, decided to speak up.

"Just make sure you stand next to him," she responded, forcing herself to laugh. "Otherwise, people will be confused."

Tell Her About It

Another sensitive issue is the engagement announcement, where mothers-in-law may take the opportunity to express their dismay to or in front of their son's fiancée. When my husband's stepbrother called to tell his mother that he was engaged, instead of offering congratulations, she launched into an extended campaign for a prenuptial agreement, with my future sister-in-law sitting right there beside him. They politely but firmly declined. A few weeks later, the family lawyer called, saying that she had been retained to handle the prenuptial as "a wedding present" to them.

Fortunately, she and my sister-in-law got along fairly well after the wedding, probably because my sister-in-law didn't hesitate to speak her mind. She also banned my mother-in-law from her kitchen. Drinking helped, too, she said.

Being of a somewhat different mind-set, I did not ban my mother-in-law from my kitchen. Of course, she had never mentioned anything about a prenuptial to me. But I don't ban anyone from my kitchen. Cook and clean away, I say. I'll be right over there in the living room with my feet propped up.

I wish I could say that my side of the family is immune to thoughtlessness, but sadly, this is just not the case. Actually, in our brood it's more like malice. When my sister married her husband, my mother was very upset—just as she was when I married my husband (even though she had never met him).[75] Unfortunately, Mother has never been one to . . . ahem . . . hold back her feelings.

---

[75]Mother has a tendency to treat people like either Princess Diana or Satan.

So when Shaun toasted his new wife during their wedding reception, no one was really surprised when Mother chimed in.

"I consider myself incredibly fortunate to be married to Laura," Shaun said at the end of his speech, which extolled the virtues of his lovely new wife.

"You sure are," snapped Mother, loudly enough for everyone to hear.

Of course, this sort of thing does run in our family. When my uncle told his mother (my maternal grandmother) about his engagement, she chose to ignore the fact that the fiancée was beautiful, kind and a talented artist. A Southern matriarch with more than a penchant for snobbery, Marmee waited until the two women were alone. Then, squeezing my future aunt's shoulder, she said, "You know, dear, he'll never stay with someone who didn't finish college."

Well, he did. My aunt and uncle have been married for more than thirty years. And my grandmother, may she rest in peace, is long gone.

A Woman Needs Love

The way I see it, the underlying problem between mothers-in-law and daughters-in-law is expectations. That, and the fact that most women are in love with their sons. Oh, they don't admit to that, of course—even the ones who don't have husbands and who are clearly drooling all over Junior. Because that would be rather sick, now, wouldn't it? After all, Freud had no idea what he was talking about with that silly old Oedipus business.

No, when mothers are in love with their sons, they prefer to call it being "close" or "best friends." But does it really take a rocket scientist to know that it's not a good idea to be "best friends" with your child? I don't care if you have a boy, a girl or a Chihuahua, it's just plain damaging for a kid to be placed in the role of confidant to an adult. Heck, it's bad enough what kids see on TV these days. Do they have to hear about their mama's personal thoughts now, too? Lordy! Talk about a one-way street to Ritalin Land.

Recipe for a Family Volcano

1 Unhappy Childhood
1 Dissatisfying Marriage (alternative: 1 Absentee Husband)
2 cups Anger
1 cup Lack of Self-Control
1 tablespoon each of Bitterness, Jealousy and Pride
1 teaspoon Narcissism
1 Son

1. Sift together all ingredients.
2. Let sit for twenty-five years.
3. Add one daughter-in-law.
4. Shake well and stand back.

Of course, if a woman has a healthy relationship with her parents and enjoys a successful, happy marriage, she's not going to transfer all that neediness onto her son. Good parents create confident, contented children. And confident, self-aware children go on to establish good marriages, which in turn foster good parenting. Just look at *The Brady Bunch*.

Likewise, unhappy children often end up in unfulfilling (if not downright abusive) marriages, which make them unwilling, unable or unaware of how to be good parents. Which creates un-happy children. And if you don't believe me, look at *One Day at a Time*. I ask you: can anyone truly blame MacKenzie Phillips for going off the deep end with Schneider as a father figure?

Now I don't know about you, but dealing with my deep-rooted emotional issues isn't exactly at the top of my to-do list every morning. And I have yet to meet a man—at least the kind of man I'd like to date and marry—who gets a kick out of exploring his childhood pain. Besides, even if we somehow figure out we're screwed up, it's not like we're going to go cuss out our mamas, though, right? Denial is not a river in Egypt, as they say.

So when a man who has an enmeshed relationship with his mother (as the shrinks call it) goes off and gets engaged or mar-ried, a little volcano starts bubbling. Well, it's been bubbling for a while, but let's say that the temperature gets kicked up a few hundred degrees. Because Mama, who up until now has been number one on the throne of her boy's affections, is about to be unseated. And this, like nothing else, is enough to make the earth tremble.

Witness how some daughters-in-law are treated at the wed-ding. One Southern Girl described how her mother-in-law re-fused to even attend. She did show up for the reception but kept moving her chair—over and over again—in order to keep her back to her new daughter-in-law.

Other mothers-in-law make inappropriate toasts at the wed-ding. One told stories about her son's ex-girlfriends, telling everyone how much she loved the previous one.

"But I guess Elizabeth will do," she said finally as the guests squirmed.

Like many mothers, my grandmother Marmee never warmed up to her daughter-in-law, and always perceived her as a rival. Nancy hardly responded to Marmee's criticism and did everything she could to win her over, but to no avail. Finally, a decade or so into the marriage, Marmee revealed her true feelings.

"The only thing that you and Charlie have, that he and I don't have," she said, during an argument, "is sex." I think that just about says it all, don't you?

Young brides are blissfully unaware of this emotional volcano threatening to blow. If you're like most, you probably expect your mother-in-law to be an ally—maybe even a second mother to you. At the very least, you see her as an important family member who will love, accept and understand you as much if not more than she does your husband. Meanwhile, back at the mother-and-son ranch, seismologists are wetting their pants with excitement.

Some say that this kind of dysfunction has an easy cure. All it takes is for the son—your new husband—to stand up to his mother. Which is tantamount to saying, all it takes is a snowstorm in South Florida. Not that it can't happen. You just can't count on it, and certainly not with any regularity.

I personally believe it's a little more complicated than that. A man standing up to an overcontrolling mother is important— very, very important. But for that to happen, your husband is probably going to need to do some serious soul-searching. And for him to be even remotely interested in doing that, things are going to need to get a little rocky on the homestead first. And then someone other than yourself is going to need to persuade your husband that the world is about to end, if he does not face these issues.

All this takes time. Usually years. Which takes us right back to expectations. In the meantime, you need to know who you're dealing with. After all, mothers-in-laws have many different personalities. Some of these personalities, in fact, are even located within the same mother-in-law.

The Top Ten Mother-in-Law Tormentors

The Liz Smith: A master of mud slinging, this gossipy mother-in-law has a juicy tidbit about everyone. Nothing is sacred—even her son's marriage. Her business is other people's business, and whatever it takes, she's going to get the goods.

Her problem: It's fun watching relationships fall apart. Especially yours.

The Diana Ross: The ultimate narcissist, this mother-in-law's life revolves around drama, beauty appointments and shopping. Your wedding? She'll try and make it back from Palm Beach—but no promises. Her roots need touching up, you know.

Her problem: It's all about her, baby. Get out of the way.

The Tonya Harding: She's mean, she's trashy and she's got a bat. Previously a star in her own right, this mother-in-law was dethroned at your wedding. Now she's out of shape and has lost all her endorsements, making her one very unhappy skater. Second place? Forget that.

Her problem: You stole her baby, and she's going to break your kneecaps.

The Queen Elizabeth: She's royal and she knows it. This blue blood has a personal assistant and can trace her roots to the *Mayflower*. Her dinner table has more utensils than a chop shop and her shoes have their own closet. As comfortable in a limo as a private jet, she prefers her martinis neat and her daughters-in-law wealthy.

Her problem: Her son is destined for greatness. You're blocking the way.

The Anna Nicole Smith: She may have started out in a trailer park, but this mother-in-law now has money—lots of it—and knows how to spend it. With a cash register for a heart, she accounts for every penny and then some. Usually acquired through marriage, her bank account is the tool with which she controls people, and she doesn't hesitate to use it.

Her problem: You've got her number—and you don't need her money.

The Whitney Houston: She used to be a sweetheart, but nowadays, cravings rule her life. Whether on booze, cocaine or prescription pills, this mother-in-law is hooked—and it ain't pretty. She'll do whatever it takes to get that fix.

Her problem: She's never met a chemical she didn't like.

The Madonna: Although this mother-in-law now wears riding clothes and glides around her country mansion serving tea, S-E-X still dominates her life. The only thing more risqué than her past is her lingerie drawer. She flirts with her son, makes embarrassing innuendos and sees every woman as competition.

Her problem: Her son is the sexiest man alive.

The Tammy Faye Bakker: Did you say makeup? Or close-up? Although this mother-in-law may not have money for food, she wouldn't dare put down her curling iron—except for dinner. And she'd rather burn one of her sequined gowns than miss a monthly hair appointment.

Her problem: You don't wear enough eye shadow. Or jewelry. Or highlights.

The Winona Ryder: She may be dainty, but this mother-in-law is sneakier than a pair of Adidas. And when it comes to the truth, she's more creative than Hollywood. Maybe it's mental illness, or maybe it's just boredom, because she certainly doesn't need to steal. But it's SO much fun.

Her problem: She likes your pearls. A lot.

The Hilary Clinton: With an Ivy League education, a power career and a highly dysfunctional marriage, this mother-in-law thrives on appearances. She's the classic overachiever who won't hesitate to tell you what she thinks—whenever and wherever. Now stand up straight.

Her problem: She's never wrong. Neither is her son.

That's What Friends Are For

Dealing with a mother-in-law is no easy task, and a number of Southern Girls have suggested strategies that might seem extreme—but only to those who haven't walked a mile in their Manolos. Alcohol and prescription drugs are the ones most frequently recommended (for the mothers-in-law, that is), especially during extended visits. Others have proposed serving food that your mother-in-law is allergic to. And then there's murder, of course, with slow-acting poison being at the top of the wish list.

Now I know this is a real bummer, but the last time I checked, the decor of my local penitentiary was somewhat tacky, and the buffet selection was even worse. So, as tempted as I am, I'm encouraging you to steer clear of the truly evil tactics. The good Lord said that He'd get revenge for us, and He has a way of being mighty creative in that department. Witness the mother-in-law who kept faking seizures during her visits. The daughter-in-law, a nurse, insisted that real grand mal seizures did not consist of batting one's eyelashes, leaning back in a chair and saying, "Oh, I'm having a grand mal seizure, y'all! Stop the car. Oh, okay. I'm better now."[76]

Her husband, however, fell for it every time. He not only believed his mother, but catered to her every whim for days after one of her "seizures." He even criticized his wife for doubting the woman. Finally, the day before dear old Mom was supposed to go home, she had a real seizure and had to be hospitalized. Then even the son was forced to admit she had been making it up. Like I said, God knows what He's doing up there—even if it doesn't always seem like it.

What's left? Well, a little wisdom from the trenches.

First, say experienced Southern Girls, having a mother-in-law is not like having a second mother. No matter how much you long for it, she will never be your mother—or anything remotely approaching a mother, for that matter. She didn't raise you, she barely knows you and she's not about to adopt another adult at this stage of her life. Accept it and move on.

Second, no matter how nice she may be, it's unlikely that your mother-in-law will ever become a girlfriend. There's your age difference, which means a generation gap. (And for any Mrs. Robinsons out there, trust me when I say that this is hardly your ticket to BFF[77] status.) There's also the lack of shared history. Friends connect because of common experiences, and the only thing you have in common with your mother-in-law is the future—not the past.

That doesn't mean, of course, that the two of you won't be friendly, and even enjoy spending time together. But even under

---

[76]Accoring to the Mayo Clinic, grand mal seizures are typically characterized by loss of consciousness, falling down, loss of bowel or bladder control and rhythmic convulsions.
[77]Best Friends Forever.

the best of circumstances, you won't be able to tell her your secrets, nor should you. In legal speak, that's what's known as a conflict of interest—a big one—and woe unto you, should you violate it. That's what friends, not mothers-in-law, are for.

With the rare mother-in-law who's actually trying to be your BFF, count your blessings that she likes you so much. Remember, too, that she's on a learning curve as well, trying to figure out how to do her job. Don't give into the temptation to treat her like a girlfriend, however, because this will backfire sooner or later. Be gracious and friendly, but set limits. When she embarks on hour-long telephone calls, casually beg off, after updating her with any news. Use caller ID. Be slow to return calls and e-mails, and accept only the occasional invitation. And don't ever share negative feelings or frustration about your husband (this is good advice with any mother-in-law), and screen what you say about even your own family and friends. Eventually, she will get the message. And if it hurts her feelings, tell yourself that you're doing the right thing—for everyone. You are.

The third piece of advice from experienced Southern Girls is to recognize that you're never going to be completely comfortable around your mother-in-law. Sure, you'll wear your pajamas and slippers in front of her someday, and maybe even nurse your baby (although probably with a blanket), but there will always be a level of awkwardness when you're together. You're both going to feel like guests in each other's home for many years, and you should behave accordingly.

In other words, you will always have to clean your house whenever she comes—and clean it well. And you should treat her like any other guest—with fresh sheets, some magazines by the bed and perhaps even a bouquet of flowers. Remember, you catch more flies with honey than vinegar. Besides, she expects to be treated like a guest, even if she doesn't admit it. Not only that, but she's also forming an opinion about you that will be shared with someone, somewhere, someday—if not everyone on the planet. So do what you can to feel good about yourself. Turn on the Southern charm, and if she doesn't appreciate it, just turn the other cheek (the one on your face, not your fanny).

Fourth, accept that your husband will always be a bit of a baby in his mother's presence. It doesn't matter how emotionally healthy we become when we leave home. As soon as we return, we revert right back to our old ways. So your husband will need to learn that you, not your mother-in-law, come first. And once he learns that, he will still need to figure out what that means. Then he'll need to work up the courage to stand up to her without alienating her. She is, after all, his mother. And he loves her, bless his little heart.

All this takes time. Lots of time. You can help the process by encouraging him to hang out with men who have overcome these hurdles, and who have healthy relationships with their wives and mothers. Seek them out, ask for their advice and spend time in their presence. Heck, kidnap them if you have to, and make them share how they finally learned to stand up to their mothers and—this is the big one—defend their wives when they came under attack. Because, as we've seen, wives do come under attack. And the only thing that's going to stop that behavior is Hubby. Until then, however, you will probably watch as your husband becomes a fearful, anxious child who defers to his mother whenever she expresses the slightest thought, frustration or desire.

Finally, don't criticize his parents to him—no matter how tacky and awful they may be. You don't like it when he criticizes yours, so extend him the same courtesy, as much as it pains you. He's just going to defend them, anyway. And that will make you mad. Again, that's what friends are for—to listen to you complain about the in-laws. Your husband simply can't do it.

My advice, when all is said and done? Go into the marriage with rock-bottom expectations about his parents. Try not to have any (or many) preconceived ideas about how you want your mother-in-law to treat you, or how much or how little your husband should stand up to her. Expect a little competition and some insensitive comments, and don't take it personally. And if things turn out well, it will be a nice bonus.

No matter what, treat her with respect. Remember, she's the fly—the nasty, ugly, annoying little fly—that you are wooing to your jar of honey, where she will get stuck and die a painful death. I mean, stop bothering you. In the meantime, when she drives you nuts, tell a friend. Or three. Blog about her. Write a book. Run for mayor. If none of this works . . . well . . . okay. If you must, go ahead and spike her food with a very mild sleeping pill. Just make sure she's taken them before, isn't allergic. Then give her only a very small dose. You just want her to be drowsy so she'll take a nap and go to bed early. Nothing more. Because, trust me—prison green is really very passé right now.

ELEVEN

Conflict Resolution: Saturday Night's All Right for Fighting

About a year before my wedding, I took a graduate class called "Building Strong Marriages in the Local Church." During the discussion time, a married couple shared their frustration with the many mundane things couples fight over. They described problems with toothpaste (rolling versus squeezing), toilet paper (under versus over) and the way that food should be placed in the refrigerator. The husband was tall, and would often miss items that his shorter wife would place on the lower shelves. She just wanted to put the food away and have room for everything.

They fought about all these issues and more, and I remember feeling incredulous. I was engaged, madly in love and looking forward to many happy years with my new husband. Those things were a cliché! Mark and I wouldn't be arguing over something as stupid as the way to extract toothpaste. On the rare occasion that we did disagree, it would be over important things—problems of great significance. Naive young thing that I was, I voiced my thoughts. The married woman said simply, "Just you wait."

Well, I have waited. More than a decade, in fact. And I'm happy to report that Mark and I have never once argued over the toothpaste, the toilet paper or the refrigerator. When we argue, we argue over problems of great significance—like the dishwasher (correct way to load it), the kitchen sink (staying dirty) and the laundry (not getting folded).

When it comes to conflict with your spouse, you never know what will trigger your rage. We've all got hot buttons. And getting married is a bit like getting into an elevator with a small child. There's a very good chance that all of 'em could be pushed at once.

If I Had $1,000,000

Early on during our first year of marriage, I happened to spot my husband hovering over the stove, making himself some Kraft Macaroni & Cheese. Now before I go any further, I must tell you that I had not yet realized the burning need for the Two-fer-One Food Rule in marriage. This rule states that for every two meals husbands make, buy or steal for themselves (typically breakfast and lunch), they get one meal made for them (typically by the wife, but not always—takeout counts, too). The Two-fer-One Food Rule is a vital part of any successful marriage, and one that soundly counteracts problems associated with Learned Helplessness, which is discussed in detail in chapter five.

At this stage, however, I was still merrily chugging along,

ruining my husband's palate for packaged food while also caving into his refined performances of Learned Helplessness. I had just spent a decade in France and French-speaking Switzerland, you see, having been dragged there by my mother and new stepfather. And it was fun—even if I did have to repeat high school in a language that I didn't speak. My absence from the United States for these years, however, played a significant role in the drama that was about to unfold.

On this particular day, I was very pleased to see Mark fending for himself (yay, Mark!). Even though I had yet to unearth the Two-fer-One Rule, I wasn't stupid. I was witnessing the Holy Grail of husbandry, and I knew it. However, I couldn't help but feel sorry for the guy, too. I had never seen Kraft Macaroni & Cheese in my entire life, and frankly, it looked positively revolting. Was this thing edible? And could I bear to let my sweetheart consume it? I opted for compromise. I would help Mark make his lunch—not make it for him. Little did I know, I was setting myself up for disaster. Fortunately, as is often the case, my ignorance saved the day.

Now you may think that making Kraft Macaroni & Cheese is simple. And for some people, I suppose it is. But having spent my entire adult life in the greatest cheese-producing country in the world, I had never seen powdered cheese—orange or otherwise. I still haven't, except in this concoction. So when Mark began boiling his pasta, I took the little package of what I believed to be "seasoning mix" and attempted to dump it into the water.

Mark jumped up so fast you'd have thought I was turning off the Super Bowl midgame. Grabbing my arm, he yelled, "What are you doing?"

"Helping you make your lunch, honey," I said with a beatific smile.

Mark wrestled the packet away from me. "You don't put that into the water!"

"Yes, you do," I insisted, holding out my hand. "That's seasoning."

Mark wrinkled his forehead. "Hello! That's the cheese!"

"Mark, please," I said, "that's not cheese. Look. It's orange powder. See?"

"It's cheese, I tell you," he said, raising his voice and holding on to the packet like a loaded gun about to misfire. "You sprinkle it over the noodles after they're cooked."

I laughed. "Mark, I am a very good cook, and I'm telling you, that is not cheese," I said. "It's some kind of orange spice, and clearly, you're supposed to put it in the water while the pasta is boiling, to flavor it. I attended Le Cordon Bleu cooking school, you know! And seasoning boiling pasta is a little trick I learned."

"Well," said my husband with a self-satisfied smirk, "you may have gone to the Cordon Bleu, but they obviously didn't teach you how to make Kraft Macaroni & Cheese!" And with that, he proceeded to strain the pasta, dump it into a bowl and sprinkle the orange mixture on top, where it instantaneously congealed into the glutinous mass that my fellow Americans call "cheese." *Quel horreur.*

Girls, I learned a lesson here. When you are so convinced you're right that you're rolling your eyes and trotting out your résumé, life may have a little surprise in store. So be humble. And don't ever interfere with the Two-fer-One Rule of Food.

You Can't Change That

When it comes to conflict resolution, there's only one problem for me and my husband. Not a big problem, mind you—just a little one. But one that has a tendency to cause just the tiniest bit of tension. This problem is that when I get mad, I tend to scream and cuss like a cowboy. Occasionally, I throw things.

I inherited these traits from my Delta-born-and-bred mama, who is completely insane, bless her heart. Mother initiated me into the fine art of feminine rage at the tender age of three. With one fell swoop, she knocked my daddy to the ground with her well-seasoned, cast-iron frying pan—something that all dutiful Southern women own and cherish. Being unconscious at the time, Daddy did not respond to Mama's shouted accusations, which inflamed her even further. After she threatened to call an ambulance, Daddy finally started to stir. To this day, I do not know whether it was co-incidence or fear over what the paramedics might think that caused him to finally get up.

Now I have no doubt that my father, who's been known to drive more than one woman crazy, probably did something heinous and deserved a good whack. Men often do. But thankfully, we don't always get what we deserve in life. Whether he did or not, however, Daddy got knocked unconscious. And thus imprinted into my toddler genetics, this lesson has been a real pain unlearning, let me tell you.

I don't want to offend anyone here, but I have a sneaky feeling that Southern Girls know exactly what I am talking about. Shrinking violets, we are not. Steel magnolias, they call us—and steel makes a mighty big bang when hit hard enough. So like many Southern Girls, I got used to raising my voice. My Yankee husband, on the other hand, has a tendency to stew. He came from a home where you could do just about anything and not get punished, much less yelled at. As polite as they can be, his family tends toward the "ignore it and maybe it will go away" theory. My family, by contrast, prefers the "beat it to death and it will go away" approach to conflict. As Florence King wrote, "Southerners have a genius for psychological alchemy. If something intolerable simply cannot be changed, driven away or shot, they will not only tolerate it but take pride in it as well." That's us. The cast-iron-frying-pan clan.

So let's just say that Mark and I had quite a few fights in those early days, and there wasn't anything "fair" about them at all—on either side. And just so you do not get the wrong impression and think that I was the only one causing problems, let me share a little delightful fact about the way that the average husband handles conflict. Uh, he doesn't.

Another Brick in the Wall

At their jobs, men can be true experts. When a problem crops up, they'll deal with it head-on. "Sorry, Bob, those specs don't fit." With friends, they won't hesitate to mention an issue. "Hey, Andy, quit leaving your smelly sweats in my car, man." Family can be tricky, but when push comes to shove, most men will step up to the plate and say what needs to be said. "Dad, we're not having kids yet, so just leave it alone."

If a potential conflict involves women, however—and by women, I mean wives and/or wives-to-be—well, you can just forget that. Men run faster than Forrest Gump from a woman who's mad at 'em. The way I see it, human problems (and are there really any other kind?) are like going to the vet, and your husband is the dog.[78] When your car pulls into the parking lot, he knows exactly what's about to happen, so he'll do everything in his power to stay in that car. You, on the other hand, will pull like crazy on his leash until you finally get his sorry butt inside. At which time he will pee on everything in sight.

---

[78]This is just an analogy. I would never imply that men are like dogs. No, never.

Men understand this dance. But they still nurture the illusion, however naive, that if they resist long enough, you'll give up, and peace will somehow flow like a river, without any interruption. But, oh, how wrong they are. Because if there's anything a Southern Girl knows, it's how to stick up for herself. Don't forget that our great-grandmothers single-handedly saved themselves—and their silver—from Sherman's savages, who committed all sorts of heinous acts, from pillaging and burning their homes to rape and even murder. The war may have been 150 years ago, but that kind of shock is not easily unlearned, I tell you. In fact, it's passed down from generation to generation, just like those traumatic experiences suffered during the civil rights period by African-Americans. So trust me when I say that no matter what her race, your average Southern Girl is not about to let any man pull the wool over her eyes.

Now I recognize that everyone is different, and I truly do not mean to mislabel those of you who happen to be conflict avoidant. I know you're out there, and I sincerely hope you're getting counseling for it, because passive-aggressive behavior can be very dysfunctional indeed. In my opinion—and this is just me—avoidance behavior is way worse than, say, just hitting a guy over the head with a frying pan and getting it over with. Which is, of course, your right and prerogative. I'm merely pointing out that passivity is not the typical attribute of a Southern Girl, who learns early on—much as I did in my mother's kitchen—that sometimes hitting somebody on the head with something very heavy can feel mighty good, indeed. Kind of clears out the old and makes way for the new, if you know what I mean.

So let's just stay that if you're like me, your dog is going to that vet. And it doesn't matter one bit if he pees on everything in sight or attacks that sweet old lady's cat. He's going inside. Men know this. The ones who married Southern Girls, anyway. And I think this is why they have a tendency to just shut down. It's an astonishing trick, when you think about it. Here they are, normal human beings (well, sort of) who can carry on a conversation (I know, just bear with me) and actually (okay, occasionally) even look you in the eye. Then all of a sudden, it's as if the body snatchers have arrived and sucked the life out of your husband, right there on that couch. He doesn't move, he doesn't say a word and no matter what you do—no matter how much you scream, cry, plead or cajole—he just stares at you like a frog on a log with those big old bulging eyes.

I have no doubt that one of these days, I'm going to arrive at the circus to see a new act: The Amazing Stoic Husbands! Step right up and pay yer money, folks! See 'em stare! Try and imagine what they're thinking! And just try and get through to them!

Of course, now, once you're hitting them over the head with frying pans, they're not saying much, either—but that's for a whole different reason.

Hard to Say I'm Sorry

A big part of men's stoicism is the inability to apologize—or at least that's what they'd like us to believe, anyhow. Elton John may be gay, but he's a man, so he knew exactly what he was talking about when he sang, "Sorry seems to be the hardest word." Because even when they're as wrong as white after Labor Day, a man will do anything in his power to avoid an apology.

One caveat. I personally believe that the reluctance to apologize goes hand in hand with passive-aggressive behavior, which I've witnessed in women, too. But since many men tend to be

passive-aggressive, this shoe fits. The underlying problem, however, is male pride, and that's something you'll be forced to deal
with all your life. Men do not like to apologize, and for the most
part, they will not apologize. It doesn't matter if has cheated at Mo-
nopoly, gotten drunk and made a fool of himself, lied about an old
girlfriend, washed and ruined your silk shirt (after you made him
swear he wouldn't) or trashed your mother's car. Apologies from a
man are as rare as steak tartare. Not only that, but the more heinous
the crime, the less likely he'll be to admit he's wrong—even when
it's so bad he's made front-page headlines, neon lights are blinking
"EVIL" and George Thorogood is striking up the band to sing
"Bad to the Bone."

How to Get a Man to Apologize

1. Do warm-up exercises with his mouth while he is
   sleeping.
2. Practice for several months, moving them into the "I'm
   sorry" position whenever needed. Forgive him for whatever he has done wrong.
3. Ignore crazy thoughts like "He doesn't mean it." He
   does. Of course he does. He just doesn't know it.
4. Once free from any anger or bitterness, explain to your
   husband the crucial link between his apologies and sex
   with you—not absolutely mandatory, but very, very
   helpful indeed.
5. Demonstrate this with a test run.

There is one strategy that you can try, however, and the earlier
the better. The ideal time, in fact, is early on in your relationship,

before he's committed any major transgressions.[79] Failing that, just begin as early as you can. You'll need to start with a few warm-up exercises.

Tonight, when your husband is sleeping, take his mouth and gently move his lips into the "I'm sorry" position. After all, saying he's sorry does involve moving his mouth, and since men talk far, far less than women, this muscle can really get out of shape. As you watch his lips saying the magic words, be sure to savor the moment. Reflect on all the things that he's done to hurt you, and accept his apology. Now move his lips into the "I'm sorry" position a second time, and feel yourself relax. Breathe deeply, and allow forgiveness to flow though you. Be sure to ignore crazy thoughts like "He doesn't mean it." He does. Of course he does. He just doesn't know it.

Now do it a third time. Isn't that better? Your husband is sorry, you've forgiven him and all is right with the world. Be sure to be very nice to him, in the morning.

Practice this exercise three or four times a night for four weeks—more if you're really angry. After a month or so, his lips should be really limber, and ready to practice a conscious apology. Next, one night when things are going well and you have some downtime, explain to your husband that you're doing an experiment. Ask for his help. Tell him that, first of all, you want him to know that you've forgiven him for all the wrongs he has ever committed. You love him, he's your husband and there is no anger or animosity whatsoever in your heart.

When he looks at you like the dog that just killed the neighbor's rooster (as mine once did), give him a hug so he knows you mean it. Next tell him that you've been doing some thinking, and that you've realized that the two of you need to have

[79]Like the first or second date.

more sex—much more. Smile when you say this, and enjoy the look of delight as it spreads across his face. When he reaches for you, give him a kiss, but hold him off. Tell him that you know how difficult it can be for him to figure out when you're in the mood—and worse still, what to do when you're not. Let him nod, then say, "But there's always one surefire way to get me in the mood, and I wanted to share it with you. Because I just know it will spice up our sex life."

Snuggle up really, really close to him at this point. Reiterate the point. As his face lights up, explain that flowers are great. You love 'em, so be sure to bring them around sometime. He'll nod. Jewelry is even better, tell him. You love that, too. So don't hesitate to indulge whenever he really wants to get lucky. He'll nod again. But more than anything, tell him, there are three magic words that you want to hear. They're the words that get you in the mood. In fact, when you hear those words, you will want to jump his bones as soon as possible.

"Three words," whisper to him. "Do you know which ones they are?"

"I love you!" he'll say triumphantly, and then no doubt try and get down to business. But this is where you shake your head. "Oh, honey. I love you, too—more than you can know," you must say. "And I do so love to hear you tell me you love me, too. Those are good words. Very good words. But there are three words which are even better. Three words that get me even more in the mood, and much faster."

Allow him to look perplexed for a moment or two, then snuggle up to him a little more, take a deep breath and say, "The three words that turn me on the most—the absolute most on the entire planet—are . . ." Pause dramatically.

"Yeah?"

" 'I'm sorry, honey.' "

"For what?" he'll say.

"No. Those are the words," you'll clarify. "The three magic words. 'I'm sorry, honey.' "

Let that one sink in. Then while you have his attention, say, "Would you like to practice?"

He'll look at you like you're suggesting a winter dip in the Chattahoochee so be sure to keep that loving look on your face. Then quickly explain that he's done nothing wrong at all. On the contrary, in fact! You just want to hear him say those words—for fun, to get you in the mood. Tonight. Right now.

Hopefully, this will do the trick, and however reluctantly, he'll eventually mutter,[80] "I'm sorry." Be sure to give him plenty of affirmation, and don't be disappointed at how quietly he says it, or how much he lacks conviction. If he's willing, have him say it a second time. Then reward him with affection. Lots and lots of affection. Because this is a learning experience for him, and you want your husband to learn well that good behavior is handsomely rewarded. In fact, you want him to be so excited about apologizing that he's not only comfortable with it, but excited about doing it. Very excited.

Remember, just like everything else in life, practice makes perfect—and teaching a man to apologize is definitely a marathon, not a sprint. The more your husband practices, however, the more likely he'll be to admit he's wrong, bring you flowers each day, perhaps a piece of jewelry, as well, and beg for your forgiveness after every single fight, without any prompting at all.

And if you believe that, then please let me know, because I've got a great deal on some Katrina-ravaged property I'd like to sell ya down South.

---

[80]Probably more softly than a mouse with laryngitis, but that's okay.

The Wanderer

One of my more significant newlywed arguments occurred prior
to our first vacation with the in-laws. We were going on a week-
long trip with Mark's family to Yosemite National Park (which his
elderly grandmother still calls "Gethsemane"). Being a new bride,
I was nervous about spending a week in a small cabin with a bunch
of strangers. Silly me.

In the rush to make the two-hour drive to the airport, neither
of us ate breakfast. It was lunchtime when we arrived, but we had
an hour before departure. The tiny airport had just one terminal,
however, and nothing to eat. So together with the friend who'd
driven us there, I decided to head back to one of the fast-food
places we'd passed on the way in.

Mark, ever the cautious one when it comes to time, warned me
not to go. "You'll miss our flight," he said, like a prophet of doom.

We argued for a few minutes, so I checked with the agent about
boarding time, which was a full forty minutes away. Convinced we
could easily make it back, my friend and I drove off. Mark even
asked me to pick up something for him, if you can believe that.

My friend and I returned in plenty of time. In fact, we were so
early that we actually laughed, saying, "Let's just stroll in, as if we
have all the time in the world." We did, after all. Our little puddle-
jumper plane wasn't even boarding for fifteen more minutes.

To my shock, however, the terminal was empty. And Mark,
my beloved, was nowhere to be found. Then I spotted our little
plane on the tarmac. The doors were closed and the propeller was
in motion.

"Ma'am?" I said, rushing over to the ticket agent and fum-
bling in my purse. "I believe that's my flight. Here—here's my
boarding pass."

"I'm sorry, but boarding is finished," she said smoothly.

"What? I'm supposed to be on that flight!" I screamed. "And my husband—have you seen my husband? He must be in the bathroom. It's the two of us, traveling together. We'll miss our flight. Please. Maybe we can page him."

"Your husband has already boarded . . ."

"I beg your pardon?"

". . . and once the propeller is in motion, no one else can board the plane. FAA regulations," she said calmly.

"What did you say?"

"It's federal law, ma'am," she repeated. "You can no longer board the plane."

"No. What did you say about my husband?" I said, my eyes bulging.

"Your husband boarded with the other passengers," she said.

It took a minute for that one to sink in. I looked down at the burrito that I'd bought for him. I looked up at the plane, outside the window. Then I shook my head. "Please, ma'am," I said, "I have to get on that plane. We're going on a family vacation. I'm meeting my in-laws. And my husband will kill me. I can't believe he left me. . . ."

"I'm sorry," she said, conveniently forgetting that she had contributed to my little problem. "There's nothing I can do."

"But you told me we'd be boarding at twelve forty-five!" I mumbled. "It's just twelve thirty!"

"On your ticket it is clearly stated that passengers must be present at least thirty minutes prior to actual departure time," she replied, and I could swear I saw a hint of glee in her eyes. "Sometimes, we leave early. Your husband did ask me to give you this, though."

And with that, she handed me my suitcase, backpack and laptop, which Mark had left behind, and returned to her work.

Numbly, I walked over to the glass window and watched the plane as it taxied down the runway, thirty minutes before its scheduled departure time. I later learned that Mark was sitting right next to a window. Had he looked up, he would have seen me. But he was way too busy reading his book.

Several hours later—after a frustrating conversation with an airport supervisor, the purchase of a new ticket, a nerve-racking flight and a world-record footrace between airport terminals—I finally caught up with my husband. Having boarded that connecting flight early (of course), he was on the last leg of our trip, still reading. And he was sitting on the aisle—my seat, according to my ticket.

"Hey."

He looked up, his eyebrows raised. "Hi," he said calmly. "You made it." I pushed past him, took the middle seat and tried not to grit my teeth.[81] "Here," I said, handing him his lunch.

He hesitated, then slowly said, "Thanks."

"It's a burrito."

Mark nodded, still watching me.

"And I hope you like it, because it was a very expensive burrito." If he hadn't been so nervous, I think he would have laughed.

My only consolation, as I watched him eat, was that the burrito was cold and had turned to mush at the bottom of my purse.[82]

---

[81] I've done a lot of that since Mark and I married, and it's become a real problem for my teeth, I tell you. I talked to the dentist about it just last week.

[82] Should this ever happen to you, by the way, please learn from my mistake and do not bust your butt chasing after the man who left you. Not only will it send him a very bad message, but it will be far better to have your fight once he gets home, rather than in front of his family, as we did. So if your husband ever abandons you in an airport, consider it God's gift and just go on home. Buy yourself some ice cream and catch up on your reading. I wish I had.

Time After Time

The $50 Burrito Story, as this incident came to be called, was not the first time that Mark and I had a disagreement over time. In fact, time is one of the things over which we argue most. Mark sees time as something concrete, as in "Five o'clock means five o'clock." Which, I guess, is logical. But I tend to see time as a bit more fluid. Sure, five o'clock means five o'clock. But who's to say it doesn't also mean five ten or five fifteen? After all, if my husband gets someplace early, why can't I arrive a little late?

People who like to be on time get extremely stressed out when they're late—and extremely annoyed, when others are. This, I'm sure you will agree, is the understatement of the year—particularly if you've ever experienced their wrath. Time-conscious people are usually task-minded individuals who believe that it's rude to make other people wait. And it is. Of course it is. After all, how hard can it be to get dressed and fed and organize one's thoughts, tasks, items and travel arrangements around one tiny little goal? They do it, and we should, too. So in order to make sure that time-conscious people are not rude to the people they are meeting—people who are often perfect strangers—they will not hesitate to be rude to you, should you get in their way. And just how logical is that? I ask you.

Those of us who are less time-conscious see things differently. We're typically overachievers who accomplish many goals during short periods of time—not because we choose to, but because . . . well . . . because we're overachievers who have a hard time saying no, quite frankly. And while our accomplishments bring us a lot of satisfaction and accolades, they also mean that we're always racing to fit everything in. Arriving early, in this context, seems somewhat absurd. I mean, think of all the things we could be doing during those extra fifteen minutes! Calls, e-mails, errands—you name it.

Not only that, but because we're highly relational people as well, we'd rather shave our heads than be rude to someone just to be on time. So, unlike the time-conscious people, we're rude to the person who's waiting for us. And just how logical is that? I ask you.

Naturally, this thinking presents most couples with a conflict—because time-conscious people usually marry non-time-conscious people, you know. Which means that one will want to go, go, go, while the other wants to tarry, tarry, tarry. I have yet to resolve this problem myself—although having small children does seem to be doing the trick quite nicely, I must say. Therefore, I can only offer some suggestions.

First of all, if you're the one who's anal about time—pardon me, I mean "time-conscious"—your only hope is deception. Speaking from the point of view of one who is hopelessly addicted to tardiness, this is not likely to change. In fact, trust me when I say that with children, it will get worse—much worse. Time is on our side, as they say. So the only thing you can do is trick your spouse into thinking he's late, when he's really on time.

There are two ways to do this, and both strategies have worked pretty well for Mark. The first is to tell your spouse that events begin before they do. My husband likes this one, because it gets him somewhere really, really early—at least five minutes before the event starts. The other way you can do this is to set every watch, pager, clock, cell phone, microwave, stove, PDA and computer that you and your husband own five to ten minutes early. Wait until he is sleeping, then do the deed. You'll be thrilled; he'll be on time.

Eventually, he will discover what has happened. But, with a bit of luck, he'll also be too busy to change them all back. And, even if he does, he'll probably miss one or two—which will mean that you can point to that clock and insist that it is the correct time.

Now if you're the one who plays loosey-goosey with the clock, it's imperative that your husband understand that the day he married you, waiting became a part of his life. A significant part. He can resist this fact. He can deny it. He can complain about it. He can yell about it. But eventually, he must embrace it. And having embraced it, the wise husband will also choose to wait in a way that is helpful—to himself, to you and thus to the world at large. I call this "constructive waiting," as opposed to "destructive waiting," which serves no purpose whatsoever—except to annoy, frustrate and possibly even enrage the person you are waiting for, and thereby delay her even further.

Destructive Waiting

- Hovering and/or loud sighing
- Drumming fingers and/or rolling eyes
- Pacing
- Asking, "How much longer?"
- Saying, "Hurry up."
- Yelling, "Hurry up!"
- Beeping horn

Constructive Waiting

- Reading newspaper
- Checking e-mail
- Shooting hoops
- Vacuuming
- Doing dishes
- Doing laundry
- Scrubbing bathrooms

Constructive waiting is waiting that achieves goals—great goals. In fact, so convinced am I of the benefits of constructive waiting that I just know that, should it be adopted by government leaders around the globe, world peace would surely follow. Activities such as reading the paper, checking e-mail and surfing the Internet come to mind. Grading papers or drafting a brief can also be good—anything work-related. Sports are also excellent activities that fall under the category of constructive waiting. Hoops can be shot, footballs can be tossed, basketballs can be bounced. TV can be watched, too, without fear of interference. But let's not forget cleaning, which is a truly wonderful activity for the husband bent on destructive waiting. After all, at any given time in a home there are always dishes to be done, floors to be vacuumed and commodes to be scrubbed. And, I ask you, now, what task-minded husband would truly want to while away precious minutes when he could be accomplishing these great things?

Baby, It's Cold Outside

As you can see, there are numerous possibilities when it comes to arguments between a husband and wife, and I'm sure you will find new and creative things to fight about, whether clichés or issues of great significance. Advice is plentiful, but so are the hormones—especially during the early years, when we're all wrestling for control. So when all else fails, and conflict erupts into full-scale battle, remember the following tips.

During particularly vocal fights, try and position your husband near an open window. You should remain on the opposite side of the room, near a closed window. That way, the neighbors will hear him yelling rather than you. Even if your husband doesn't yell, with a bit of luck they'll still think it's him—especially if you lower your voice a few octaves.

Also, after screaming at your husband or insulting him, be sure to add, "Bless your heart," so he'll know you still love him. Finally, when throwing things, avoid lightweight objects. You want to go for things that will really knock him out cold. That way, he won't remember what happened—which means you can tell him later on that you won the argument.

If all else fails, you can always lock him outside the house. That's what my mother did, to not one but two husbands. Both were in their underwear, and it was late at night, during the winter. Which, I admit, is rather harsh. But, hey, at least they didn't get the frying-pan treatment.

TWELVE

Birthdays, Anniversaries and Special Events: I'm Gonna Make You Love Me

When I was a little girl, I remember sitting with my mama as she played "Someday My Prince Will Come" on the piano. We were visiting my grandmother in Charlotte, North Carolina, and it was springtime. A breeze drifted in through the open window and a bouquet of fire orange lilies sat on the mantel, artfully arranged in a hundred-year-old cut-glass vase that had been a wedding present to my great-grandmother and namesake, Anne Bell Brandau. Several years later, that precious heirloom would be smashed to smithereens by a husband and a wayward ball that should never have been together, in a living room, to begin with. But on that day, I was enjoying the moment, watching my beautiful mama sing the song inspired by my favorite fairy tale.

Even though I was just four, I recall being struck by two

things. One, how unbelievably bad Mama's singing was. Two, I had a prince—and he was coming! Just like my father, who had sent my mother those beautiful flowers, my prince would give me gifts, too. He would wait on me, dote on me, cherish me and spend his life trying to please me. And of course, he would always remember my birthday.

Wouldn't It Be Nice

Now memory, I've learned, is a funny thing—especially if you're a man. Sometimes it works and sometimes it doesn't. And, like most things husbands do wrong, they're not usually about to fall all over themselves apologizing. Witness the spouse of one Southern Girl, who insisted, after overlooking their anniversary yet again: "I didn't forget. I just didn't remember."

I have been fortunate. Unlike other "princes," mine has yet to forget any special days.[83] He also does pretty well in the gift department, so I count myself among the blessed. But every husband has his flaws, and nonremembering husbands could be one of the things you face, post-honeymoon. There are worse things, though. Well, actually, come to think of it, forgetting your birthday is pretty bad, now, isn't it? Bottom of the old barrel.

But take heart. Once you've been married a few years, your husband will definitely remember important dates with increasing accuracy. The reason for this is a special hormone that begins to form in the male brain on his wedding day. Called Yerupacreek-withoutapaddlebuddy, its purpose is to trigger an early-warning

---

[83]Except Mother's Day, 2005.

system—much like the buoys floated out to sea to warn coastal dwellers of incoming tsunamis.

Release of this hormone starts small. But, unlike memory, it stays in the male brain, so that the longer a man stays married, the more Yerupacreekwithoutapaddlebuddy he will have. A husband of five years, for example, will sense that an important event is approaching—although he may not know what or when that event is. His thought pattern will therefore sound like "There's something I'm forgetting." A man who has been married for ten years will discern the nature of a looming event, but not necessarily be able to pinpoint the date. His thought may be "I think my anniversary is soon." A husband of twenty years, by contrast, will know with certitude that his wedding took place in June ("Or was that her birthday?").

Release of the Yerupacreekwithoutapaddlebuddy hormone also swells with each oversight and/or misstep that a husband makes. The more public the lapse—and the more tears shed—the greater the output. It is further augmented by hateful stares and comments from mothers- and sisters-in-law. Although it can take years for this hormone to build up to sufficient quantities so as to be exclusively relied upon, major errors trigger exponential release as well, increasing future likelihood of disaster warning. Missing an anniversary, for example, tends to double its release. Forgetting a wife's birthday quadruples it. And overlooking Christmas may mean hospitalization for the husband—if not due to the hormone spiraling out of control, then because of his wife's reaction.[84]

Yerupacreekwithoutapaddlebuddy is not infallible, however, and it takes years to work effectively. In the meantime, you will want to limit your pain and suffering.

---

[84]Please note that should a divorce occur, all quantities of Yerupacreekwithotapaddle-buddy are immediately expelled from the male system.

Do You Remember?

One of the great things about living in the age of technology is . . . well . . . technology. When it comes to remembering birthdays and anniversaries, it is definitely a man's best friend—which means that it is our best friend, too. Just like those who man the help desk, our modern-day heroes, so are the gadgets they work with. And while I'm on the subject, may I take this opportunity to thank Bill Gates, Steve Jobs and every other geek on the planet[85] for their infinite wisdom and intelligence, which so few of us appreciated in high school. We bow in humility and we ask—we plead!—for your forgiveness. You are the gods of technology upon which our very lives depend, and if any of us had been bestowed with even half a brain in high school, we would have swished our ponytails at you, oh, you back-pocket carriers of slide rulers, and not the quarterbacks who are now selling vacuums for a living.

But tragically, having lost that golden opportunity to become your brides, we nevertheless remain indebted to each and every one of you for life. Because of you, our computers run. Because of you, our cell phones function. And because of you, our husbands will never again forget our birthday or anniversary.[86]

Never mind that technology doesn't come cheap, girls. Because even though this remedy involves cold cash—warm credit cards, actually—it is truly infallible. I ask you, women of the jury, what would it be worth for your husband to (a) remember every special event for the rest of your life and (b) give you the perfect gift for each and every one of those special events?

---

[85]Minus the scumbag spammers and sleazeball inventors of viruses, trojans, worms, adware and spyware, of course.

[86]And if they do, they certainly won't have a decent excuse.

I rest my case.

Your secret weapon in this mission is called a Blackberry, a wonderful wireless device that combines a phone, organizer, e-mail and Internet access into one amazing little device. You must shop for and purchase a Blackberry for your husband. Yes, I know you'd like one, too, but the Bible does say that, without knowledge, people perish. And your husband desperately needs knowledge, because without it, he will perish—probably at your hands. Happily, a Blackberry will solve this problem, because it can be preprogrammed with all of your husband's need-to-remember dates. This includes everything from birthdays and anniversaries to the first day you met and the first day you kissed, to the last day he opened the car door for you (if you can remember).

Do you see where I'm going with this? If you're willing to invest just a little time and money, and if your memory serves you well—and if not, just be creative—after bestowing your husband with this all-important piece of technology, you will be the recipient of numerous gifts. So get your little gizmo and go to work.

Don't limit the programming to just dates, however, which will leave dear Hubby with a terrible dilemma about what to buy. For each occasion, make sure to add the gift that you would like for him to purchase, along with all the pertinent information he will need to buy it. For example, June 23 might read *1st Wedding Anniversary: Buy David Yurman Gold Dome Bracelet at Mayors Jewelers, 3225 Peachtree Road North East, Tel. 404-261-4911, Open Mon–Sat, 10 a.m. to 6 p.m., closed Sundays.*

Also, be sure to use a tickler system, beginning three to four weeks out, with regular reminders. If you haven't already discovered, men can be quite stubborn. And it goes without saying that you will need to act both surprised and thrilled when your gift finally arrives.

Although I don't recommend it, some of you may truly prefer

to be surprised when it comes to the selection of your gifts. If this is the case, God go with you, and you will need to resort to the more tried-and-true method called "hinting."

Ain't Too Proud to Beg

Gift giving is second nature to Southern Girls, because we love to shop. And, oh, how we luuuuuuuv to shop. We also enjoy making friends and family feel appreciated, and buying that oh-so-special item for every person on our list—plus one or two for ourselves, of course—is a great way to do that. For most men, however, the thought of finding a suitable present for a wife is akin to planning a strategic hunt for the northern hairy-nosed wombat.[87] Fear and anxiety will not prevent husbands from hunting for a gift, of course, because (a) they know they must and (b) they like hunting. But it's not like men have ever received training in this complicated science, bless their little hearts. So newly married Southern Girls would do well to be patient—while also bracing themselves for cheap, tacky and wholly inappropriate gifts.

I am not sure why, but men love to give kitchen gadgets to their wives. Maybe *Leave It to Beaver* marathons are required viewing after football games or something, but the fact that most young brides don't know the difference between a can opener and a corkscrew doesn't factor into their thinking, either. And we're not talking about that gorgeous fire engine red KitchenAid Professional Plus stand mixer that retails for more than our monthly food bill, okay?[88] We're talking about run-of-the-mill

[87] One of the rarest mammals on earth, reputed to number less than one hundred.
[88] Hint, hint, honey.

items like spatulas, garlic crushers and toasters that most of us would barely buy for ourselves, and which force us to smile like we're in the dentist's chair after we open them.

I did hear about one Southern Girl who received a brand-new, state-of-the-art washing machine for Christmas.[89] On the other hand, I also heard about a husband who gave his new wife an iron and ironing board. "But it's a female power tool," he stammered when she stormed out of the room. "And I'd love to get a power tool for Christmas!"[90]

These items, which can actually be used (albeit to serve and wait on Lover boy), are nothing compared to the brain-numbing gifts from some husbands, however. One Southern Girl received a tarantula for her birthday. To be fair, this was in West Virginia. But you gotta love her husband's excuse. "You said you wanted something furry and cute from the pet store," he cried when she started shrieking.

Another Southern Girl received a shrunken head. Her spouse claimed that he had bought it to commemorate their honeymoon in the Amazon. Still another made the annals of moronic behavior when he presented his wife with a cemetery plot. To this day, he isn't sure whether she was more upset by the fact that he purchased it from his mother or the fact that the wife's plot happened to be right next to the mother-in-law's.

Husbands also tend to be very creative when it comes to disguising things they've purchased for themselves as "gifts." More than one Southern Girl has opened a beautifully wrapped box only to discover a drill, a screwdriver or some other Home Depot tool du jour. Items from military and hunting catalogs come under

---

[89] And if you're going to insist on the whole kitchen-gadget thing, then this is infinitely preferable to plastic mixing cups.

[90] And I'm sure she'd love to give him one, too—right over the head.

this designation, too—and, no, it doesn't matter that the wife may have mentioned she likes camouflage. Oh, and look out for the garden equipment. One Southern Girl received a lawn mower—after weeks of begging her husband to cut the grass.[91]

Sports gear also comes under the duplicitous heading. Unless you've just qualified for the U.S. Olympic team, you will need to inform your husband that volleyballs, hockey sticks and basketballs simply do not qualify as gifts. A new pair of skis and a vacation for two in Aspen, on the other hand, definitely do. Clothing with team logos is out-of-bounds as well, along with game tickets—unless they're for the Super Bowl, when your hometown team is playing.[92] But don't let him go too far down this road. I heard of one man who gave his wife a coupon for a long weekend in Canton, Ohio—complete with tickets to the Pro Football Hall of Fame. May he rest in peace.

Finally, there are the embarrassing gifts, in which underwear and bathing suits play a starring role. We appreciate the thought, boys, but we'll just keep our fanny and boob sizes to ourselves, thank you very much. Oh, and anything from a porn store? Don't even go there.

The grand prize for appalling gifts, however, goes to the guy who gave his wife a douche kit for Christmas. Yes, a douche kit. Not only that, but this thoughtful gentleman presented it to his bride while visiting her family—at the same moment that his sisters-in-law were unwrapping mink coats and pearl necklaces from their husbands. His perplexed excuse when she burst into tears? "But you said you needed one!"

So, as you can see, you should consider yourself lucky if your

---

[91] Is that passive-aggressive or what?
[92] Southern Girls do so love football.

next visit from Santa yields a pasta roller. But don't neglect the power of the hint. Therefore, whenever you go out with your husband, you should be on the lookout for suitable gifts. After spotting something you like, drag him over to the store window to see it. It will not be enough to state how much you appreciate this item, however. You will need to get his undivided attention and state specifically, while looking him in both eyes, "Oh, I would do naked backflips if I got that bracelet for Christmas!"

When he stops daydreaming and says, "What? What did you say?" repeat the comment. Repeat it again. Then raise one eyebrow and add, "Naked. Wearing nothing but that bracelet." With a little luck, the next day, he'll at least remember that there is something you want—and that you'll wear it and only it—even if he can't recall exactly what that is.

Next find the item in the store's catalog. Make a dozen copies of the page (color is best) and circle the item, adding the words: *What I Want for Christmas This Year!* Leave one copy on his desk, fax one to his office and paste another one on the mirror where he shaves. Then begin mailing them to him at the rate of one per week until the week before the event.

If possible, you will want to locate the item online as well. That way, in addition to the hard copy reminder he receives in the mail, you can also send him weekly e-mail reminders with hyperlinks to the item. I have found this to be particularly effective. If time is of the essence, you can always resort to last-minute messages on his cell phone. And for something really important, ask your mother to leave a message. But save this for something really special, like your promotion, which will be unexpected and therefore completely off the gift radar.

Meanwhile, here's a little questionnaire that you can clip and give to dear Hubby. He should put it in his wallet, next to your photo, and use it whenever he has the urge to surprise you with something. And if he doesn't have your photo, then let that be your next present to him.

Troubleshooting for Husbands: How to Determine If Your "Gift" Is Really a Gift

1. Is it any of the following: a new car, a fur coat, diamond jewelry or a sizable gift certificate to your wife's favorite store?

    Yes. Congratulations! It's a gift. You may stop the questionnaire.

    No.

2. Is it something your wife has specifically requested for this day?

    Yes. Congratulations! It's a gift.

    No.

3. Did you purchase it at a florist?

    Yes. Congratulations! It's half a gift.

    No.

4. Will you ever use this gift?

    Yes. It is not a gift. It is a present for yourself.

    No.

5. Does it plug in?

    Yes. Skip to Question 7.

    No.

6. Does it contain technology?
   Yes. Skip to question 8.
   No.

7. Can it be used to accomplish any form of cooking or cleaning?
   Yes. It is not a gift. It is a household item.
   No.

8. Can it be used for work or for any income-producing activity?
   Yes. It is not a gift. It is a business expense.
   No.

9. Did you purchase this item in a reputable store or on a respected Web site?
   Yes.
   No. It is not a gift. It is a pawnshop item.

10. Is it expensive?
    Yes.
    No. It is not a gift. It is a thoughtful gesture.

11. Is it jewelry?
    Yes.
    No. Skip to Question 14.

12. Was this jewelry given to you by a family member?
    Yes. It is not a gift. It's a hand-me-down.
    No.

13. Can it be returned?

>   *Yes*. Congratulations! It's a gift.
>
>   *No*. It is not a gift. It's a donation for the Junior
>   League silent auction.

14. Is it clothing?

>   *Yes*.
>
>   *No*. Skip to Question 19.

15. Does it have a sports-team logo on it?

>   *Yes*. It is not a gift. It is memorabilia.
>
>   *No*.

16. Is it lingerie?

>   *Yes*.
>
>   *No*. Skip to Question 18.

17. Is it edible?

>   *Yes*. It is not a gift. It is dessert.
>
>   *No*.

18. Did you have to guess her size?

>   *Yes*. It is not a gift. It is Russian roulette.
>
>   *No*.

19. Does it involve a trip?

>   *Yes*.
>
>   *No*. Skip to Question 22.

20. Will anyone you know, besides your best friends, be on
    this trip?

>   *Yes*. It is not a gift. It is a family reunion.
>
>   *No*.

21. Are any of the following involved in this trip: beach, lake, mountains, roaring fireplace, four-poster bed, breakfast in bed?

    Yes. Congratulations! It's a gift.

    No. It is not a gift. It is a night in a hotel.

22. Does it contain sugar?

    Yes.

    No. Skip to Question 25.

23. Will she have to bake or cook it?

    Yes. It is not a gift. It is dinner.

    No.

24. Is it chocolate?

    Yes. Congratulations! It's a gift.

    No.

25. Does it involve sports?

    Yes. It is not a gift. It is a night out with the guys.

    No.

26. Has your wife ever expressed interest in this gift?

    Yes.

    No. It is not a gift. It is gambling.

27. Is it plastic surgery?

    Yes.

    No. It must be something very weird. Return to store, purchase a new item and retake questionnaire.

28. Are you willing to accompany your wife to the hospital,
    wait in the waiting room during her plastic surgery
    operation, stay by her side after the surgery without
    watching sports on TV, then bring her flowers and
    anything else she requests while also nursing her back to
    health and/or hiring someone else to do so, for as long
    as she needs—for not only this hospital visit but any
    forthcoming one as well?

    > *Yes.* Congratulations! It is a gift.
    >
    > *No.* It is not a gift. It is irreconcilable differences.

Signed, Sealed, Delivered

I don't know about you, but like the hippies from the sixties, I believe in flower power. As in, the power of a flower to brighten your
day and make everything okay. Alas, only the rarest of women
will receive regular blossoms from her hubby. So Southern Girls
may want to take things into their own hands. After all, we deserve to receive the very best, now, don't we?

Select a nice florist and pay them a little visit. Then walk
around the shop and peruse the catalogs until you have chosen
several lovely (large) bouquets. Instruct the florist to send them to
you on the relevant dates—everything from your birthday and
anniversary to all the holidays. Don't forget minor ones, like
Cinco de Mayo, Flag Day and Canadian Thanksgiving. After all,
it's his credit card you'll be paying with. Prepaying, to be precise.

Next you will want to take home a stack of note cards. Spend a
little time filling them out with romantic, loving sentiments that
you long to hear from your husband. Don't hold back—the more
romantic, the better. When you are finished, hand them over to
him to be signed. Then return the notes to the florist and ask that

they be attached to the flowers, in no particular order. You'll want to be surprised, after all.

When the flowers arrive with the notes, be sure to tell your husband how much you appreciate them. Yes, I know. It's not quite the same thing as him going out on his own and buying them. But look at it this way, darlin'. One, you're getting something—and that sure is better than nothing, right? Two, if your mother starts griping about him, show her the flowers. Finally, revel in the fact that your husband is feeling pretty doggone guilty right now. Which means he just might go out on his own and get you something next time.

In the meantime, enjoy the flowers. Oh, and the ones my daddy sent to my mama that spring day so many years ago? Little did I know, but we weren't visiting my grandmother. We had moved in, because Mama had left Daddy. She had done so honorably, of course—by loading up her brand-new station wagon with clothes, china and the wedding silver, then sneaking away while he was at work. Far from being a romantic gesture, therefore, the flowers were a desperate one. Let's hope you never find yourself in that situation—with or without an antique cut-glass vase.

THIRTEEN

Babies: In the Year 2525

When Mark and I were engaged, we used to laugh when our parents discouraged us against having children right away. "Don't rush it," they advised, trying to cover their anxiety. "Plenty of time."

Good advice. After all, Mark and I had known each other for less than a year when we got married, and we needed time to solidify our relationship. We wanted to enjoy each other, have some fun. No problem there. But, oh, how quickly their tune changed. "You don't want to wait too long for kids," they said just months after our honeymoon. "You never know."

We smiled. They were sweet. They wanted grandchildren. And we wanted kids—at least four. We loved children. But we were young. We were having fun. And we had all the time in the world.

As the years passed, we kept telling each other the same thing—
even as our friends warned us. "It's not as easy as you think," they
said. "We know a lot of couples your age struggling with infertility."

Thanks, we said. But we weren't ready yet. We had to finish
school first, pay off the student loans. And we really wanted to
buy a house. Save some money. You know, move ahead in our
jobs. And, gosh, we so enjoyed sleeping late on Saturdays. Reading the paper in bed on weekends, leisurely drinking lattes. Going
for bike rides. Having friends over. Oh, we were young. We had
plenty of time.

Six years later, still somewhat reluctant, we decided we'd better start. We got pregnant on the first try—just like they said we
would back in sex ed. See? What was the big deal? We were excited but terrified. Were we ready? Could we do this? We could!
We told everyone we knew. We started buying baby clothes. We
discussed names.

A few weeks later, I miscarried. The experience was similar to
a bike wreck. Not a car accident, where paramedics arrive and by-
standers gawk, but one of those crashes everyone has as a child.
One minute, you're pedaling against the wind, the sun warming
your face, your hands stretched out in a balancing act you've done
so many times before. The next you're sprawled on the ground,
knees skinned and bloody, your only means of transportation destroyed. You're injured but not mortally, bleeding but not se-
verely, and strangely, oddly alone.

With a miscarriage, nobody sends flowers, nobody comes to
visit. People say it's for the best, it wasn't meant to be, you can try
again. They expect you to be up and about, and barely miss work.
They change the subject. It's not so much the pain but the disappointment, the isolation and the fact that people treat it not as a death
but a loss, as if you've merely misplaced something you can easily
find again.

After our miscarriage, Mark and I were intensely aware of how real our baby had been—and how very much we wanted it. We grieved as only parents can grieve.

My obstetrician was blasé. "Don't worry," he said. "It's common. Just try again."

It took seven months before we could try again. And then, once again, we miscarried. We were horrified. Had we waited too long?

"No," said my new obstetrician, in soothing, doctor-knows-all tones. "You're still young. Plenty of women have babies well into their forties these days."

He's right, of course. Plenty of women do have babies after forty. But how many is plenty? I've begun to ask. And how many miscarriages, tests, artificial inseminations and in vitro fertilizations do these women have to go through to get those babies? How many suffer from genetic or chromosomal disorders, because they were born to older mothers? And how many couples have been relegated to just one or two children when they longed for three or four?

Everywhere I looked, friends, neighbors and coworkers were having problems bearing children. Not women in their twenties or very early thirties (minus a few exceptions), but almost every women I met who was thirty-five or older (minus a few exceptions) was either struggling to conceive or miscarrying repeatedly—if not both. I later learned that they have a word for women thirty-five and older, in obstetrical circles. It's called "advanced maternal age."

I'd woken up. I was smelling the ovulation. And it was not the sweet scent of ease and simplicity that I had been promised, while I blissfully pursued my career.

"Give it to me straight," I said to the first of three infertility specialists I would eventually consult. "You can't find anything wrong. Why am I miscarrying?"

She hesitated.

"I'm tired of the hype," I insisted.

The doctor licked her lips, then said slowly, "Your eggs are old."

"I'm thirty-five."

"Right. Sometimes, at your age, it takes a few tries to get a good one."

A second fertility specialist said the same thing, so we kept trying. We had two more miscarriages. Then finally, amazingly, we got a good egg. Our daughter was born when I was thirty-six. Words cannot describe the joy we had in holding her, feeding her, showing her off to a world that affirmed that she was just as beautiful, brilliant and well-behaved as we knew her to be. We reveled in our newfound status as Mama and Daddy.

Somewhere in between nursing and potty training, though, we knew we should be plowing ahead. But if there's anything we have learned throughout this process, it's how unbelievably dense we were. We waited almost two years before trying again. We had two more miscarriages. One of them was twins.

A friend younger than I but with similar struggles recommended her specialist. I made an appointment, filled out the mountain of paperwork and once again submitted to all the tests. I told my new doctor about the "old eggs" diagnosis. Did he agree?

"Absolutely," he said. "A woman is medically considered to be 'subfertile' at age thirty-five."

Which means?

He showed me some charts. If I had tried to get pregnant again at thirty-six, my chances of conception would have been 15 percent. That's on any given day, the sperm meeting the egg, just like they taught us back in high school. But now, at age thirty-eight, my chances had decreased to a mere 12 percent. A 2 percent drop, in less than twenty-four months. It was shocking, to say the least. Where had this information been lurking? And what about the fifty-nine-year-old who had given birth to twins that year?

I could barely bring myself to ask my next question: what if I waited another two years?

My chances of conception would again drop, he said—this time to 10 percent, and less with each year. Add to that the risk of miscarriage, which was heightened because of my history to approximately 50 percent. And then, of course, there was the ongoing risk to the baby of Down syndrome and other chromosomal abnormalities, already elevated but poised to skyrocket, as soon as I hit forty.[93]

I felt like I'd been punched. What had I been doing while my fertility raced down this black-diamond slope? Certainly nothing that was going to cuddle me or comfort me in old age.

"You're one of the lucky ones," my doctor said. "You conceive easily. It just may take a few more tries."

In other words, if I was willing to have more miscarriages, I would probably conceive and carry to term. He offered to do in vitro fertilization—at $20,000 per procedure. But at thirty-eight, my chances were only 50 percent. He liked my idea of a fertility drug—one of the milder ones. We tried it. It made me sick, but it helped me conceive and carry to term. Last year, I gave birth to another precious child, who brings us as much love and joy as the first.

Lord willing, we would also like a third child. We wanted at least four, but sadly, that's now impossible. We waited far too long. Three, however, we might be able to do. Might. Our biggest

---

[93]The baby of a thirty-year-old woman runs one chance out of 885 of having Down syndrome. The baby of a forty-year-old runs a one in 109 chance. This doesn't include chromosomal disorders, which are even more prevalent than Down syndrome, after forty.

problem, ironically, is dealing with uninvited comments from family members who mean well when they advise against it, but don't understand how radically our perspective has changed.

Because you see, as long as we both shall live, Mark and I will regret—in that heart-squeezing, breath-robbing, tearfully envious way that only regret can bring—that we listened to the lie. Babies, we have learned, in one of the most painful lessons of our lives, are not a burden. No matter how challenging, how expensive, how inconvenient or how sleep-wrecking they may be, they are not cumbersome. They are a blessing. An amazing, life-altering, wondrous gift that should never be rejected, no matter when or how they come.

So what does this mean for you, dear newlywed couple, struggling to make a decision about when to start your family? Honestly, I do not know—and I would not presume to tell you even if I did. Having a child is an intensely personal decision that can only be made with your husband, taking into consideration your own set of circumstances. Your age, how long you've been married and your financial situation are certainly things you must consider. But don't forget to calculate the intangibles. The age you'll be when your kid goes to college, gets married, starts having babies. The importance, for your children, of having not just parents but also grandparents—and maybe even great-grandparents—to know and love. And what it would be like for your children to care for you, an elderly parent, while still in their thirties—or, worse still, live their lives without you.

These are all consequences we did not imagine, which are now very real for us. Not only that, but to adequately describe the effect of six miscarriages on our marriage would take an entire book. In our grieving, we've confronted the whole spectrum of emotions—everything from denial and depression to anger—and needed some very expensive counseling as well. Not exactly a prescription for surviving the newlywed years, if you know what I mean.

So, dear Southern Girls, please ponder the decision of reproduction with great care. And don't be misled by wishful thinking, no matter what its source.

The Future's So Bright, I Gotta Wear Shades

Now, if by any chance I am already preaching to the choir—in other words, you are good and ready to conceive—then congratulations, and let the fun begin. Sometimes, however, the old husband needs a little persuasion. So first, check out the research and show him the stats. It's out there and it's real, and it won't take much to unearth it. Second, talk to people who have struggled with infertility. Ask what they've learned, and what they would do differently. Ask how it has affected them.

Third, find some babies and children to hang out with, especially if your husband doesn't know any. Sometimes, seeing is believing, so the more adorable, the better. Just be sure to pick ones who are well-behaved—which unfortunately can seem as rare as a low-fat Krispy Kreme donut. I don't know why, but making kids obey has gone completely out of style. But sweet kids are out there. You just have to find them.

Fourth, if your husband is worried about money (and what man isn't?), try and spend time with families who have bridged the financial gap after kids. Find one that seems both happy and successful, and ask them how they do it. These days, even staying home with the kids is not nearly as impossible as it might seem. I earn more money working from home than I ever did in my full-time newspaper job, and the number of women who run home-based businesses, job share and telecommute is growing every year. Some families even survive on one salary, simply by cutting back. It takes creativity and dedication, they say, but it is possible.

Finally, remember that men feel incredibly anxious at the thought of providing for a child—both emotionally and financially. Even if you intend to keep working, children do mean additional expenses. It may take time for your husband to adjust to the idea of starting a family. So keep talking, and brainstorm together about ways you can make it work.

Top of the World

While you and your husband are pondering, thinking and praying about when to get pregnant, you can always go the extra mile. One of the best-kept secrets on the planet is how wonderful sex is when you're trying to make a baby. Just ask any parent who has knowingly (and willingly) participated, and you'll hear how romantic it can be. In fact, to underscore this point, you may want to show your husband some of the best "baby-making positions." You know, in the living room, in the Jacuzzi, on the dining room table.

Oh, I know, I know. Even with the rejuvenation that baby making will bring to your bedroom, convincing a man to start his parental engine often takes more than just sex—however high you may swing from your chandelier while having it. So here are some real ways to speed this process along.

First and foremost, be aware that men love the thought of impregnating a woman. They're just afraid of how it will all play out—and how they will support that child. The way to get around this is to talk about your husband's "seed." Men adore this concept. Actually, they not only love the concept but the seed itself—not to mention the organ that creates the seed. In fact, "love" may be putting it much too lightly. "Worship" is more like it. So the more you talk about him spreading his seed, the more interested he will be in doing just that.

You, on the other hand, may have to overcome your disgust at that sort of terminology. One Southern Girl described what happened when her husband finally told her he was ready to start a family. He wanted her to become the mother of his children, he whispered.

"I was so excited I wanted to rip his clothes off right there in the car," she said. As they started kissing, however, he made the mistake of talking about "rooting his seed."

"Leave it to a man to ruin a good thing by opening his mouth," she rightly observed.

So when talking about this concept, you may want to keep your thoughts at bay. But honestly, there really is nothing more effective when it comes to convincing a man that it's time for a baby. And if you don't believe me, just watch one announce that his wife is pregnant. It doesn't matter if it's the first or the fifth child, that guy will be strutting around like the barnyard rooster, his chest puffed up with pride, as if he and he alone has done the miraculous deed.

Another strategy involves stroking your husband's ego, which is important anyway. Remember, these boys get kicked around a lot in life, and they don't have girlfriends to build them up, like we do. (At least, we hope they don't.) So men really need all the affirmation you can dole out. And if the feminist in you balks, just view it as encouragement—something everyone requires for emotional survival. Then set about telling your husband how wonderful, brilliant, handsome and powerful he is. Is it any wonder, therefore, that you want to create another human being exactly like him? Trust me, it will be very hard for a man to say no to this kind of logic.

Next talk about the need for your husband to carry on his name, and the great legacy he will be imparting to his descendants.

If he's not into genealogy, this might be the time to embark on a new course of study. Encourage him to imagine the future as a patriarch. Abraham, Isaac and Jacob. It has a nice ring, doesn't it?

If none of this works, just talk about his seed—the almighty seed. Because, when it comes to staying sane after you've caught your man, children are definitely the next step. They're the slice of lemon in your sweet tea, the key lime in your pie and the precious little umbrella in your marital margarita—and you do not want to go through life without 'em.

The End

If you've made it this far, Southern Girl, I have no doubt that sanity is just around the corner. Figuratively speaking, of course. Because no matter how brilliant and wise you may be (and I have no doubt whatsoever about those qualities in you because you did, after all, buy this book), you've got to be just a little bit crazy to make a marriage work. I definitely am—just ask Mark. But then again, I have been all my life. Marriage just upped the ante a little.

It's not an easy thing to get your head around, this marriage business. Just remember, however, that like life, it meanders up and down, through the lowest of valleys and the highest of peaks—and it probably always will. I compare it to hiking the Appalachian Trail. Some days, the weather is so clear you can see a hundred mountaintops. The sun is blazing from a crisp blue sky, and the foliage quivers with life. You navigate the terrain and your soul sings with promise. At night, you sleep deeply, then awake refreshed. Every day is a new adventure, just waiting to unfold.

Other times, however, the fog clings to your legs like a wet blanket, making you hesitate with every step. The path that was so visible before now leads you into the brush again and again, where poisonous insects and plants await. You can't seem to avoid the rainstorms, which drench your gear and your spirits. Your muscles tremble. Your body aches. At night, you shiver, wondering what in tarnation you've gotten yourself into.

But if you dare to persevere, eventually you'll catch a glimpse of hope rising over the hills of this well-traveled path. The night comes swiftly and fills the air with bone-chilling cold, to be sure. But even during your darkest hour, there are places of refuge among the pines and crackling fires to warm your soul. You are not alone. Countless travelers have gone before you, and countless more will come.

So sit for a spell and rest your weary legs. Understanding, forgiveness and joy often come in the morning. Frequently, they come from fellow travelers. Southern travelers. And Southern Girls.

So stay sweet, y'all—and stay married. We Southern Girls are counting on you.

ANNABELLE ROBERTSON is a born-and-bred Southern Girl who has survived more than twelve newlywed years. A North Carolina native, she grew up around the South, then attended university and law school in Europe. She practiced international law before moving to Vancouver, BC, where she met and married her husband, Mark, an emergency room chaplain who recently went active duty with the United States Air Force. For the past ten years, the Robertsons have lived in Atlanta, Georgia, where Annabelle is a regular contributor to a wide variety of publications, including *Atlanta Woman* magazine and the *Atlanta Journal-Constitution*. They have two children—both Southern Girls. Visit her at www.Annabelle-Robertson.com.